SQL for Everyone

A fast and easy track for beginners that covers Oracle, MySQL, Microsoft SQL Server, Microsoft Access, IBM DB2, PostgreSQL, SQLite, and MariaDB SQL implementations

RIAZ AHMED

SQL for Everyone

Copyright © 2015 Riaz Ahmed

All rights reserved.

ISBN-13: 978-1-329-21880-2

No part of this publication may be reproduced, stored in a retrieval system or transmitted in any form or by any means, electronic, mechanical, photocopying, recording, scanning or otherwise, except as permitted under Sections 107 or 108 of the 1976 United States Copyright Act, without the prior written permission of the Author.

Limit of Liability/Disclaimer of Warranty: The author make no representations or warranties with respect to the accuracy or completeness of the contents of this work and specifically disclaim all warranties, including without limitation warranties of fitness for a particular purpose. No warranty may be created or extended by sales or promotional materials. The advice and strategies contained herein may not be suitable for every situation. This work is sold with the understanding that the author is not engaged in rendering legal, accounting, or other professional services. If professional assistance is required, the services of a competent professional person should be sought. The author shall not be liable for damages arising here from. The fact that an organization or Web site is referred to in this work as a citation and/or a potential source of further information does not mean that the author endorses the information the organization or Web site may provide or recommendations it may make. Further, readers should be aware that Internet Web sites listed in this work may have changed or disappeared between when this work was written and when it is read.

Trademarks: Oracle is a registered trademark of Oracle Corporation. All other trademarks are the property of their respective owners. The author is not associated with any product or vendor mentioned in this book.

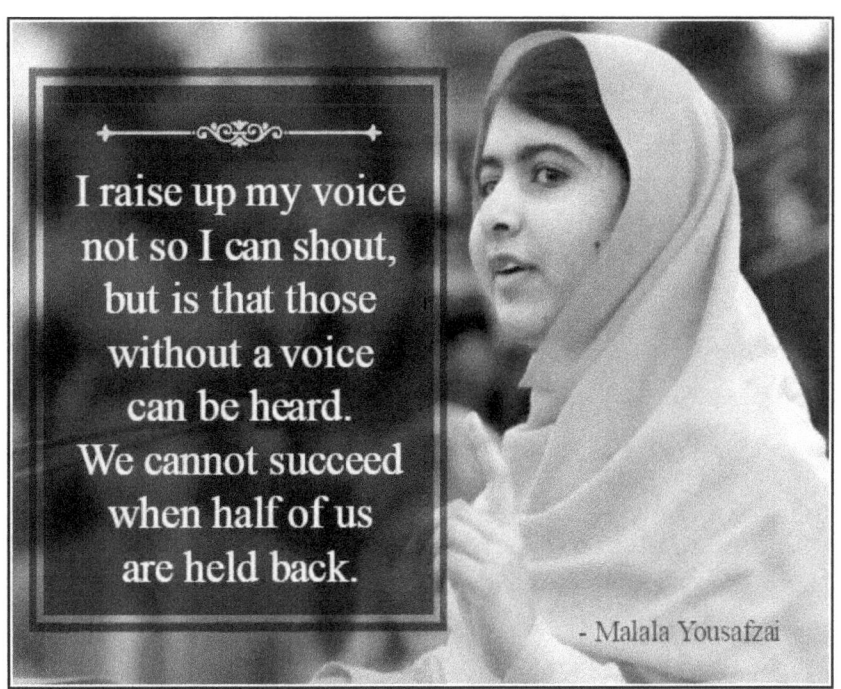

Dedicated To The Courage Of The Girl Who Stood Up for Education.

CONTENTS

Essential Database Concepts

- Introduction 2
- Who is this book for? 3
- Database and Database Management System 3
- Database Tables and Relationship 4
- Primary Key 4
- Foreign Key 4
- Composite Key 4
- Data Type 5
- Data Integrity 5
- What is SQL? 5
- Data Definition Language (DDL) 6
- Data Manipulation Language (DML) 6
- Data Control Language (DCL) 6
- Data Query Language (DQL) 6

Setup Practice Environment

- Download, Install, and Test Oracle XE Database 10
- Download and Install SQL Developer 11
- Creating Connection in SQL Developer 13

Retrieve Data From Database

- How data is extracted from databases? 16
- The SELECT command 16
- Selecting all data from a table 17
- Fetch data from selected columns 18
- Using Arithmetic Operators 19
- Arithmetic Operator Precedence 20
- Precedence with Parentheses 21
- Change Column Headings 22
- Joining Columns 23
- NULL Values 25
- Replacing NULL Values Using NVL Function 26
- Preventing Duplicates with DISTINCT 27
- Multiple Distinct Columns 28
- Sorting Records 29
- Comparison and Logical Operators with Precedence Rules 30
- Filtering Data with the WHERE Clause 32
- Comparing Character Strings in the WHERE Clause 33
- The BETWEEN Operator 34
- The IN Operator 35
- The LIKE Operator 36
- The IS NULL Operator 38
- The AND/OR Operators 39
- Add Comments to SQL Statements 42

Transform and Summarize Data with Functions

Functions in SQL 46
CONCAT Function 47
INITCAP Function 48
LENGTH Function 49
LOWER Function 50
NVL Function 51
SUBSTR Function 52
UPPER Function 53
ROUND Function 54
TRUNC Function 55
Date Time Functions 56
Date Manipulation Functions 57
MONTH_BETWEEN Function 59
ADD_MONTHS Function 60
NEXT_DAY Function 61
LAST_DAY Function 62
Conversion Functions 63
DateTime Data Types and Elements 64
TO_CHAR(datetime) Function 65
TO_CHAR(number) Function 66
TO_NUMBER Function 67
TO_DATE Function 68
Calculating Dates 69
Aggregate Functions 70
AVG Function 71
COUNT Function 73
MIN and MAX Functions 74
SUM Function 76
Aggregate Functions Used Together 77
The GROUP BY Clause 78
Using WHERE and GROUP BY Together 80
The HAVING Clause 81

Subqueries

What are Subqueries? 86
Understanding Subquery Process 87
Handling Multiple Row Subquery 88
Using Multiple Subqueries in a SELECT Statement 89
Subquery in the HAVING Clause 90

Query Data From Multiple Tables

Referential Integrity in Relational Databases 94
What is a JOIN? 95
EQUIJOIN 96
INNER JOIN 97
OUTER JOIN 98
Joins vs. Subqueries 99

Creating Tables

- What is a Table? 102
- What are Data Types? 103
- How to Create Tables? 104
- What are Constraints? 105
  - NOT NULL Constraint 105
  - UNIQUE Constraint 106
  - PRIMARY KEY Constraint 107
  - FOREIGN KEY Constraint 108
  - CHECK Constraint 110
- Create a Table 111
- Create Table from Another Table 112
- ALTER TABLE 113
  - Add Column 113
  - Modify Column 114
  - Delete Column 115
  - Rename Column 115
- Renaming Table 116
- Add Constraint After Creating a Table 116
- Drop Constraint 117
- Enable/Disable Constraint 118
- Renaming Constraints 118
- Remove a Table 119

Manipulate Data in Tables

- What is Data Manipulation? 122
- Add Data 122
  - Insert a Complete Row 123
  - Insert a Partial Row 124
  - Insert Rows from Another Table 125
- Update Data 126
- Delete Data 127

Other Database Objects

- Database Objects 130
- What are Views? 130
  - What are views good for? 130
  - Create a View 131
- What are Indexes? 132
  - Create an Index 133
- What are Stored Procedures? 134
  - Create and Execute a Stored Procedure 135
- What are Triggers? 138
  - Create and Fire a Trigger 139
- Conclusion 141

APPENDIX

- Answers to Test Your Skill questions 144

About the Author
INDEX

PREFACE

Why buy this book? Like many people, I also ask this question before spending my hard-earned bucks. In the existence of free web material and many well-written comprehensive books, this question gets more weight. SQL is older than most of us, so I can't claim to be conveying some extraordinary stuff through this book. What makes this title unique is its slender size. If you are looking for a real compact practical guide on SQL, then this book is for you. For beginners, I have tried to confine an ocean to a bucket in order to equip them with SQL knowledge in the shortest time possible.

SQL language is too voluminous and exposure of every aspect of this huge language is a very tedious task. Keeping aside the least utilized features, this book is rolled out to focus on the more operational areas of the language. It is meant to help you learn SQL quickly by yourself. It follows a tutorial approach wherein hundreds of hands-on exercises are provided, augmented with illustrations, to teach you SQL in a short period of time. Without any exaggeration, the book will expose SQL in record time.

The book explicitly covers a free platform of the world's number 1 DBMS to expose SQL: Oracle Database Express Edition. I have chosen Oracle XE because it is free to develop, deploy, and distribute; fast to download; and simple to administer. The second important reason, that might attract you as well, is that it comes bundled with Oracle Application Express (APEX), a rapid application development tool for creating internet facing applications that can be accessed via desktops, laptops, and mobile devices (such as smart phones and tablets). Once you have become proficient with the SQL language on this platform, you can easily explore other platforms on your own.

In addition to Oracle, the following renowned database management systems are also covered:

- MySQL
- SQLite
- Microsoft SQL Server
- IBM DB2
- Microsoft Access
- PostgreSQL
- MariaDB

This book is ideal for self-study, and it can also be used as a guide for instructor-led classroom training. This book is designed in such a way that you can learn SQL even if you do not have access to your PC. At the end of each chapter in this book, a section named "Test Your Skill" is provided, which evaluates the knowledge you gained in each chapter. This work is an attempt to cram the most useful information about SQL into a compact guide to put your exploration vehicle in the top gear.

Good Luck!

- Riaz Ahmed
Author

Essential Database Concepts

Chapter 1 – Essential Database Concepts

Introduction

Like many people, you might be a self-learner who likes some practical stuff to explore a technology. Although it's a little painful route, you can get through it and achieve your milestone if you possess strong determination and are fortunate enough to get some real good material on the subject. In this publication I've tried to save your precious time by providing such hands-on stuff on SQL. I won't take you in the past to tell something that is of no interest to you today (at least as a beginner). But, felling the necessity, I'll provide a little background of SQL and will cover some preliminary concepts that you must know. This chapter will really pay off if you grasp the basic concepts about database and SQL.

First of all, let's come to the word SQL. Many people say that this acronym stands for "Structured Query Language", and some are of opinion that it should be read individually as "ess-que-el" or as "sequel". Leaving this debate aside, let's see why and when this useful language was initiated. In June 1970, Dr. E. F. Codd published the principles of the relational model, wherein he proposed the relational model for database systems. Along with definition of the relational model, he also suggested a language called DSL/Alpha for data manipulation in database tables. After the release of Codd's paper, IBM formed a team to build a prototype of DSL/Alpha based on Codd's proposal. The team got success in this endeavor and developed the first version named SQUARE, which finally got the name SQL.

While SQL has become a very stable language today, you must know that all SQL implementations are not created equal. Almost all database vendors support the latest SQL standard (published by American National Standards Institute – ANSI), but most vendors have added extensions to make their implementations more powerful or easier to use. These extensions are fairly similar across different platforms, and once you have become proficient with the SQL language on one DBMS platform, you can switch to other platforms without any difficulty. For your convenience, I've explicitly covered a free Oracle platform in this book besides the following database management systems. I have provided specific instructions for these platforms, where needed.

- Oracle
- MySQL
- Microsoft SQL Server
- Microsoft Access
- IBM DB2
- MariaDB
- PostgreSQL
- SQLite

This book is meant to help you learn SQL quickly by yourself, therefore, you'll be provided instructions to set up free Oracle environment on your own PC to execute hands-on exercises for learning purposes.

Who Is this Book For?

- It is for you if you are new to SQL.
- It is for you if you are looking for a fast track to explore SQL.
- It is for you if you want to learn SQL without someone's help and in your own environment.

Before we roll up our sleeves and get to work, it is necessary to have some basic knowledge of database and related concepts first.

Database and Database Management System

We interact with many databases in our daily lives to get some information. For example, a phone book is a database of names and phone numbers, and an email list is a database of customer names and email addresses. A **database** can simply be defined as a collection of individual named objects (such as tables) to organize data. File cabinets used in an organization that carry folders and name tags are examples of paper database. From technology viewpoint, this kind of organized information handling is performed by special computer software, called **database management system (DBMS)**. And just as file cabinets come in many different colors and sizes, each DBMS available today has its own characteristics. A good understanding of these characteristics will help you make better use of your DBMS.

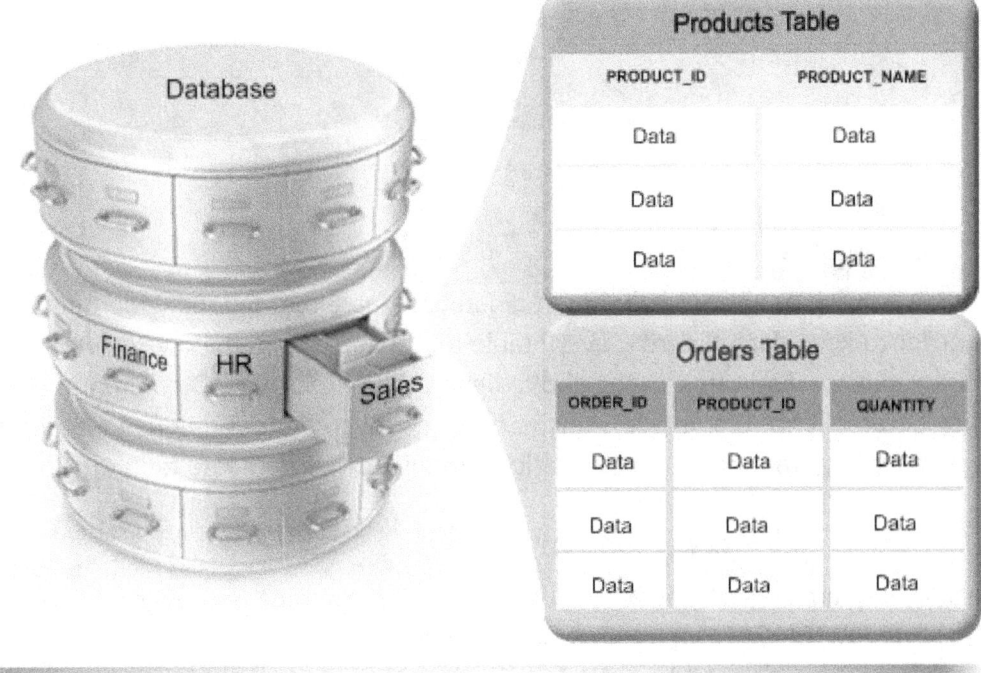

Database, Schemas, and tables

- A **database** is a container that holds various schemas (sales, hr, finance, etc). A **schema** (e.g. Sales) is a collection of individual named objects, such as tables, indexes, views, triggers and so on.
- Related data is organized and stored in **tables** such as Products, Orders, Customers etc. A table is similar to a spreadsheet, containing rows and columns.
- **Data** is stored under relevant columns in a table. For example, all order numbers are stored in the Orders table under the Order_ID column.

Database Tables and Relationship

A relational database organizes data in tables under individual schemas. Each table comprises columns and rows. Columns report different categories (headings) of data, and rows contain the actual vales for each column. Relationship among database tables is formed with the help of Primary, Composite, and Foreign keys. The following figure illustrates an example of a related database containing two tables.

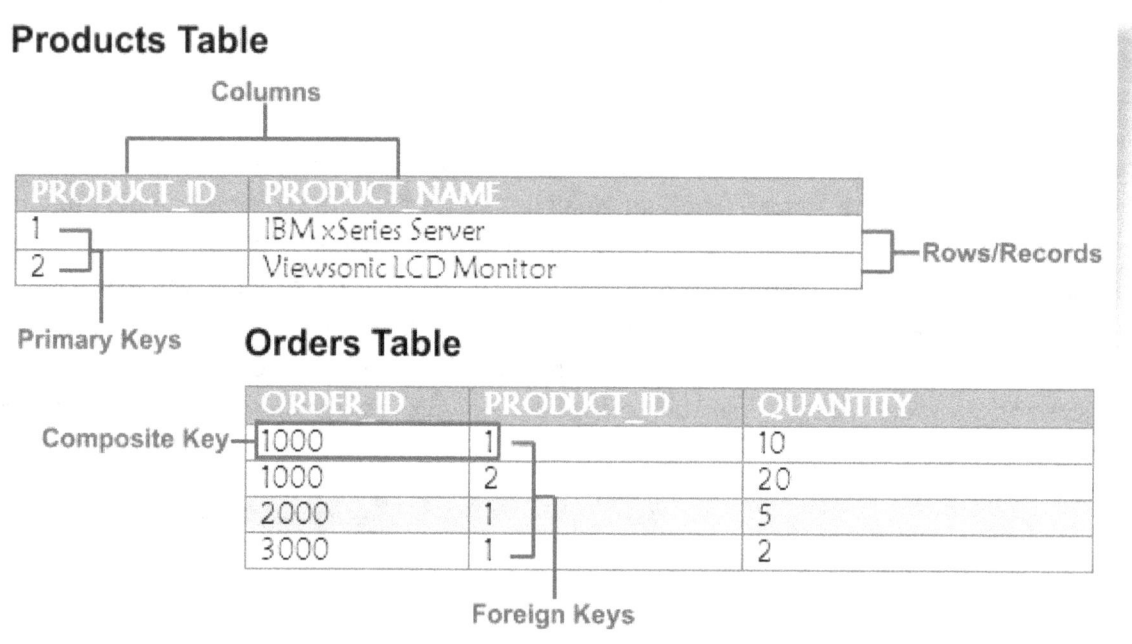

A related database with two tables

Primary Key

A primary key is a column or a set of columns in a database table that uniquely identifies each record in that table. In order to keep data integrity, every table must have a primary key. A primary key cannot be NULL and must not allow duplicates. In the above figure, the PRODUCT_ID column in the Products table is a primary key because it holds a unique value for each product. Besides unique identification of records, values in the primary key are used to create relationship with other database tables.

Foreign Key

You create relationship among database tables using matching columns. The above figure displays how PRODUCT_ID 1 and PRODUCT_ID 2 in the Products table relate to ORDER_ID 1000 in the Orders table. A primary key column in another table which creates a relationship between the two tables is called a foreign key. PRODUCT_ID is a foreign key in the Orders table. The foreign key value must exist in the table where it is a primary key. For instance, if you try to add a new order for PRODUCT_ID 4, the insert process will fail because there is no primary record for PRODUCT_ID 4 in the Products table.

Composite Key

It is a set of columns in a table combined together to form a unique primary key. As you can see in the above figure, the first two records in the Orders table carry 1000 for both records, so the ORDER_ID value is not unique for these records. However, combining ORDER_ID and PRODUCT_ID columns will create a unique primary key for the Orders table, which is called a composite key.

Data Type

Each column in a table has an associated data type which specifies what type of data the column can contain. For example, if the column were to contain a number (quantity of items in an order), the data type would be a numeric data type. If the column were to contain dates or text the appropriate data type would be used to store data accordingly. You select relevant data types to also restrict the type of data that can be stored in a column (for instance, to prevent recording of alphabetical or special characters into a numeric column). See Chapter 7 – Creating Tables, for more information on data types.

Data Integrity

By implementing the following four integrity constraint types, you ensure that your database is in a correct and consistent state.

- **Entity:** This constraint type defines a primary key which should not be NULL and must contain a unique value.
- **Referential:** It relates to foreign keys, which must match a primary key in another table, or be NULL.
- **Column:** Values in the column must adhere to the defined data type. For example, a numeric column must not contain any alphabet.
- **User-defined:** This includes compliance of data with the defined business rules. For example, customers' credit limit should be less than or equal to 5000. It is implemented using the CHECK constraint.

See "What are Constraints?" on Page 105 for further details.

What is SQL?

SQL is a command language that you use to interact with databases. It provides you with a simple and efficient way to read and write data from and to a database. It is used in two different ways: embedded or interactively. In the former case, you embed SQL commands in a program created in a different programming platform (such as Java). In the later scenario, you enter SQL commands using your keyboard on a SQL command prompt or in a GUI software (such as SQL Developer), to get your desired information on your screen. This book is intended to deal with the later scenario where you'll be taught how to communicate with databases interactively.

Normally, the SQL language is divided into the following four command categories:

- Data Definition Language (DDL)
- Data Manipulation Language (DML)
- Data Control Language (DCL)
- Data Query Language (DQL)

Chapter 1 – Essential Database Concepts

Data Definition Language (DDL)

The SQL data definition commands allow you to create, modify, and delete **objects** of a database. Typical database objects include tables, views, procedures, users, triggers and so on. Almost all SQL data definition commands start with one of the following three keywords:

CREATE: To add new database objects such as tables, users etc.
ALTER: To modify the structure of an existing database object
DROP: To delete a database object

Data Manipulation Language (DML)

This category of SQL commands allows you to change the **contents** of your database. For this purpose, SQL offers three basic data manipulation commands:

INSERT: To add new rows (records) into a table
UPDATE: To modify column values of existing rows
DELETE: To delete rows from a table

Data Control Language (DCL)

Data control commands are used to **control access** to different database objects (tables, views and so on). Data control commands include GRANT and REVOKE.

Data Query Language (DQL)

This category has just one command, but is the most significant one: SELECT. It is the sole command in SQL which is used to **retrieve (query)** data from a database.

Well, that's it for now. You have been briefed about some of the most important concepts in the world of database. You will revisit these concepts in upcoming chapters, because the information provided in these minute sections need a permanent place to sit in your minds.

Test Your Skill

1. What is a database?

    a. It stores data.

    b. It carries tables and other objects.

    c. It is a container that contains schemas, tables, and other objects to store data.

2. What is a schema?

    a. It is a database object.

    b. It is a logical area in a database created for each user to store tables and other database objects.

    c. It is a box in a database which holds objects.

3. What is a table?

    a. It contains data.

    b. It is a database spreadsheet.

    c. It is a database object which stores data in rows and columns for a particular category.

4. What is a table column?

    a. It represents data category in a table.

    b. It identifies a row.

    c. It stores data.

5. What is a row?

    a. It contains actual values for each column.

    b. It represents columns in a table.

    c. It is a table component.

6. Relationships among database tables are established using:

    a. Primary Keys

    b. Foreign Keys

    c. Both

7. The basic purpose of creating a Primary Key is to:

    a. Make a table unique.

    b. Make a column unique.

    c. Make a row unique.

8. A Foreign Key is created in a table to:

    a. Create relationship with table rows.

    b. Create relationship with parent table(s).

    c. Create relationship among databases.

Chapter 1 – Essential Database Concepts

9. Data Types are defined to:

    a. Specify what type of data a column can contain.

    b. Form table structure.

    c. Create a new table.

10. New objects in a database are created by using:

    a. DML

    b. DDL

    c. DCL

11. The SELECT SQL command is used to:

    a. Insert new data.

    b. Update existing data.

    c. Query data.

12. Identify command category (DML, DDL etc.):

    a. Revoke _____   d. Alter _____   g. Insert _____

    b. Delete _____   e. Update _____   h. Create _____

    c. Drop _____   f. Grant _____

13. Identify Primary Key and Foreign Key columns for the following tables:

Locations	Key	Departments	Key	Employees	Key
location_id		department_id		employee_id	
location_name		department_name		employee_name	
		location_id		department_id	

Setup Practice Environment

You will perform all the exercises provided in this book on your own computer. For this purpose, you have to download couple of free software: Oracle Database Express Edition 11g and Oracle SQL Developer. You need to open a free Oracle account on Oracle's site to do the download.

Download, Install, and Test Oracle XE Database

Oracle Database Express Edition (Oracle Database XE) is an entry-level, small-footprint database. It's free to develop, deploy, and distribute; fast to download; and simple to administer. Follow the instructions mentioned below to download and install Oracle XE Database.

1. Enter the following address in your browser to download the database:
   http://www.oracle.com/technetwork/database/database-technologies/express-edition/downloads/index.html
2. Accept the License Agreement.
3. Click on the *Oracle Database Express Edition 11g Release 2 for Windows x32* link, (if your PC is running 32 bit Windows operating system) otherwise, select the version compatible with your OS.
4. Enter your Username and Password. If you don't have an account, sign up for a free Oracle Web account and repeat the download process.
5. Save the zip file to your computer.
6. Once downloaded, extract the .zip file, and launch the Setup file from the extracted Disk1 folder to start installation.
7. Follow the on-screen instructions to complete the installation.

> **NOTE**
> During the installation process you are required to enter and confirm SYSTEM user password. Provide a password that you can easily remember – I set it to *manager*. This account is used underneath to test database connectivity. The final installation screen will show a port number – which is usually 1521. Network request is passed to a database through this port. Note down this number, as it is required in the next section.

The XE database installation process creates entries in the program group as show in the following figure.

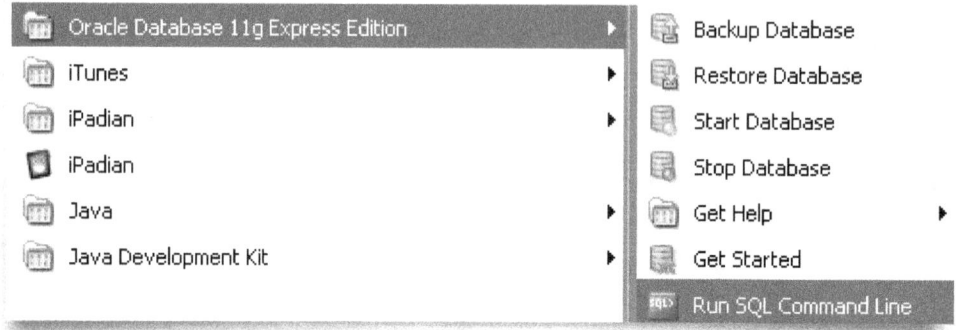

Test your database installation by clicking the **Run SQL Command Line** option. On the SQL prompt type: **connect system/manager** and press enter. If everything went well during the installation process, you'll see **connected** message on the subsequent line, which indicates that your database is up and ready to take requests. Type **exit** and press enter to quit the command line interface.

Download and Install SQL Developer

SQL Developer is a graphical user interface (GUI) tool that Oracle Corporation supplies to query databases, browse objects, execute reports, and run scripts. It supports Windows, Linux, and Mac OSX. SQL Developer is a non-licensed (free) product. Besides Oracle database, it can be used to connect and access third-party (non-Oracle) databases, such as MySQL, Microsoft SQL Server, Sybase Adaptive Server, Microsoft Access, and IBM DB2. Note that SQL Developer doesn't need any installer so it also does not create any registry entries. Similarly, deleting the SQL Developer directory removes it from your system and you do not have to run any uninstaller for it.

1. You can download it from the following URL.

   http://www.oracle.com/technetwork/developer-tools/sql-developer/downloads/index.html

2. Click the ⬇ Download link defined next to the prompt: SQL Developer requires JDK 7 or above.

3. Save and extract the zip file to a directory of your choice..

4. Double click **sqldeveloper.exe** file from the extracted folder to start SQL Developer.

> **NOTE**
> One of the first tasks that you may be prompted to do when you start SQL Developer for the first time is to locate the Java Development Kit (JDK). SQL Developer requires JDK 7 or above. If you selected the option to download SQL Developer with the JDK, then java.exe will be included in the jdk sub-folder where you extracted the zip file. If you couldn't locate the jdk sub-folder then you have to download and run the jdk software (jdk-7u71-windows-i586.exe) from:
> http://www.oracle.com/technetwork/java/javase/downloads/jdk7-downloads-1880260.html
>
> | Windows x86 | 127.78 MB | ⬇ jdk-7u71-windows-i586.exe |

Chapter 2 – Setup Practice Environment

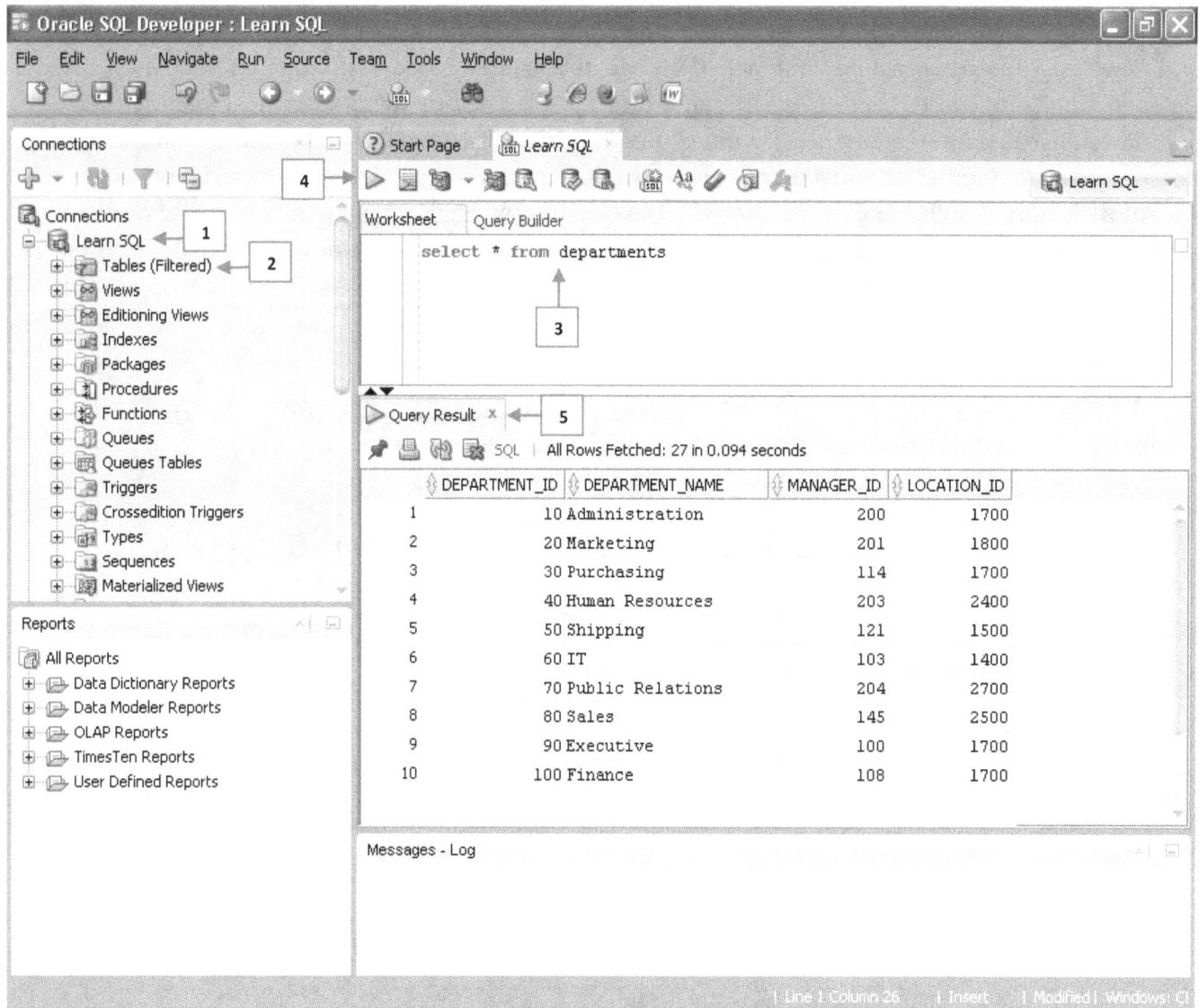

SQL Developer's Interface

The above figure illustrates the interface of SQL Developer, marked with some important sections of this useful software that you'll use in this book.

1. **Learn SQL:** The connection pane displays all connections you've created to connect to different databases. In the next section you'll create a connection named Learn SQL to connect to the Oracle XE database, that you just installed.
2. **Tables:** As a beginner you'll interact with database tables in this book to learn SQL. Once you connect to your database, you can expand this node to browse all the tables in the database. You can even see structures of tables and the data stored in each table through this node.
3. **Worksheet:** This is the pane which you'll use throughout the exercises presented in this book. Here you'll enter SQL statements to interact with your database.
4. **Run Statement:** You click this button to execute your SQL statements.
5. **Query Result:** The result of the executed SQL statement that you enter in the Worksheet will appear in this section.

Creating Connection in SQL Developer

A connection is a SQL Developer object that specifies the necessary information for connecting to a specific database as a specific user of that database. You must have at least one database connection to use SQL Developer.

1. To create a new database connection, right-click the **Connections** node Connections and select **New Connection** (I named the new connection: Learn SQL (see tag number 1). Fill in the connection form as shown in the following figure.
2. Enter **hr** for both username and password. HR is a sample schema, provided with XE database, containing tables and other objects. You'll use the data held in this schema to perform all the exercises provided in this book.
3. After completing the form, click the **Test** button. The Success message in the status section should come up, indicating that you are ready to proceed further.
4. Click the **Save** button to save the connection. The new connection should appear in the left pane of the form.
5. Click **Cancel** to dismiss the connection form.
6. Click on the **SQL Worksheet** icon and select **Learn SQL** from the provided list. This will open a worksheet for the selected connection, where you will enter your SQL statements to interact with the corresponding database.

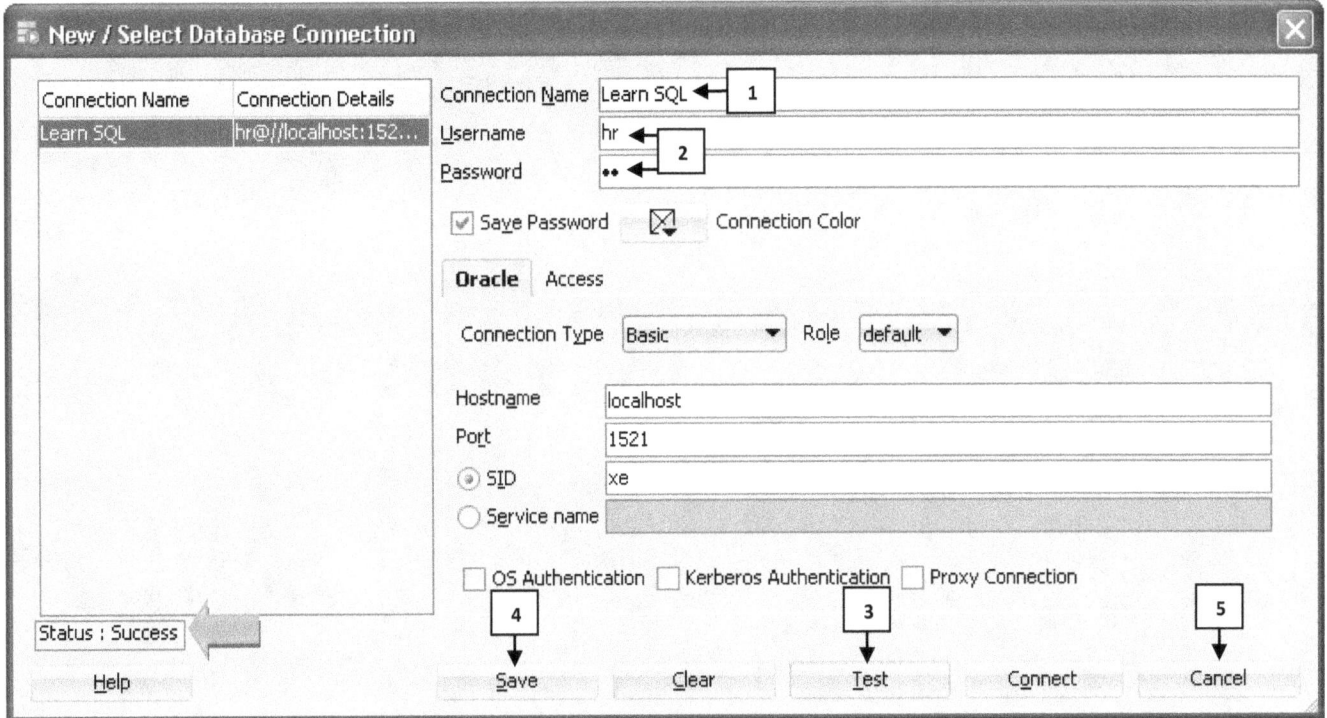

Database Connection Dialog Box in SQL Developer

That's it! You've grasped the most basic concepts about database and SQL, and have also setup the environment for the practice sessions coming ahead. Rest of the chapters in this book will walk you through to practically explore SQL, starting with the data query command.

Chapter 2 – Setup Practice Environment

Test Your Skill

1. Name any three DBMSs (other than Oracle) which are supported by SQL Developer.

    a. _____   b. _____   c. _____

2. What information do you provide when you invoke SQL Developer for the first time?

    _____

3. Besides SQL Developer what is the other utility in your current practice environment to interact with the database?

    _____

4. You need to provide information for the following six fields when you connect to an Oracle database from SQL Developer:

    a. _____   d. _____

    b. _____   e. _____

    c. _____   f. _____

Retrieve Data From Database

3

Chapter 3 – Retrieve Data From Database

How Data is Extracted From Databases?

You use SQL's SELECT command to extract data from your database. This command helps you fetch the desired data set, as well as specify the presentation order. In this chapter, you'll execute all the options of this command to fetch data from the database.

Before you proceed, go through the following guidelines to write valid SQL statements that are easy both to read and to edit.

- SQL commands and statements are case insensitive.
- You can enter SQL statements on one line or can split them on multiple lines.
- Command words can neither be split across lines, nor can they be abbreviated.
- You can use tabs and indents for better readability.
- Place a semicolon (;) as a terminator before you execute a statement (not required in SQL Developer GUI).
- In SQL syntax, text defined under square brackets [ ] is optional, and that mentioned under curly braces { } is mandatory. Keywords (such as SELECT, FROM etc.) are presented in upper case letters, while user provided values (column/table names, conditions etc.) are displayed in lower case.

The SELECT Command

Syntax

```
SELECT     [DISTINCT]  {* | column [alias], ...}
FROM       {table name}
[WHERE     condition(s)]
[GROUP BY  expression]
[HAVING    group condition]
[ORDER BY  {column, expression} [ASC|DESC]];
```

> **NOTE**
> In Chapter 1, you were introduced to the four command categories of SQL that you'll go through in this book, starting with SELECT, the sole data query command.

Syntax Explained

Clause	Explanation
SELECT	It's a keyword followed by at least one column from the desired table.
DISTINCT	It's an optional clause which suppresses duplicates.
*	Asterisk is a wild card character which is used to select all columns from a table. The vertical bar sign (|) means that you can use either * or specific column(s).
column [alias]	A list of specific column(s) of a table with optional custom headings.
FROM table name	It is the name of table you wish to fetch data from.
WHERE condition(s)	By using this clause you specify the desired data. The condition can have column names, expressions, and comparison operators.
GROUP BY expression	It divides the rows in a table into smaller groups.
HAVING group condition	Used in conjunction with GROUP BY, it is used to return only those groups which are specified in the condition.
ORDER BY	With this clause you specify the display order of the fetched data set.
ASC|DESC	Orders the fetched rows in ascending or descending order.

Selecting All Data from a Table

You can use the SELECT command in its simplest form to retrieve all data from a table. For this purpose you use the asterisk (*) character to fetch data from all columns. In the following example, the SELECT statement requests data from all columns in all rows contained in the Departments table. Assuming that you're connected to the HR schema using the *Learn SQL* connection, enter the following statement in the Worksheet pane – as shown in the figure below – and click the **Run Statement** ▷ button. The Query Result pane will appear, carrying the result for the executed query.

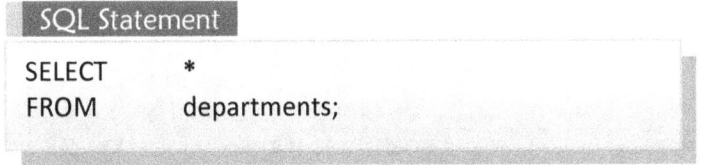

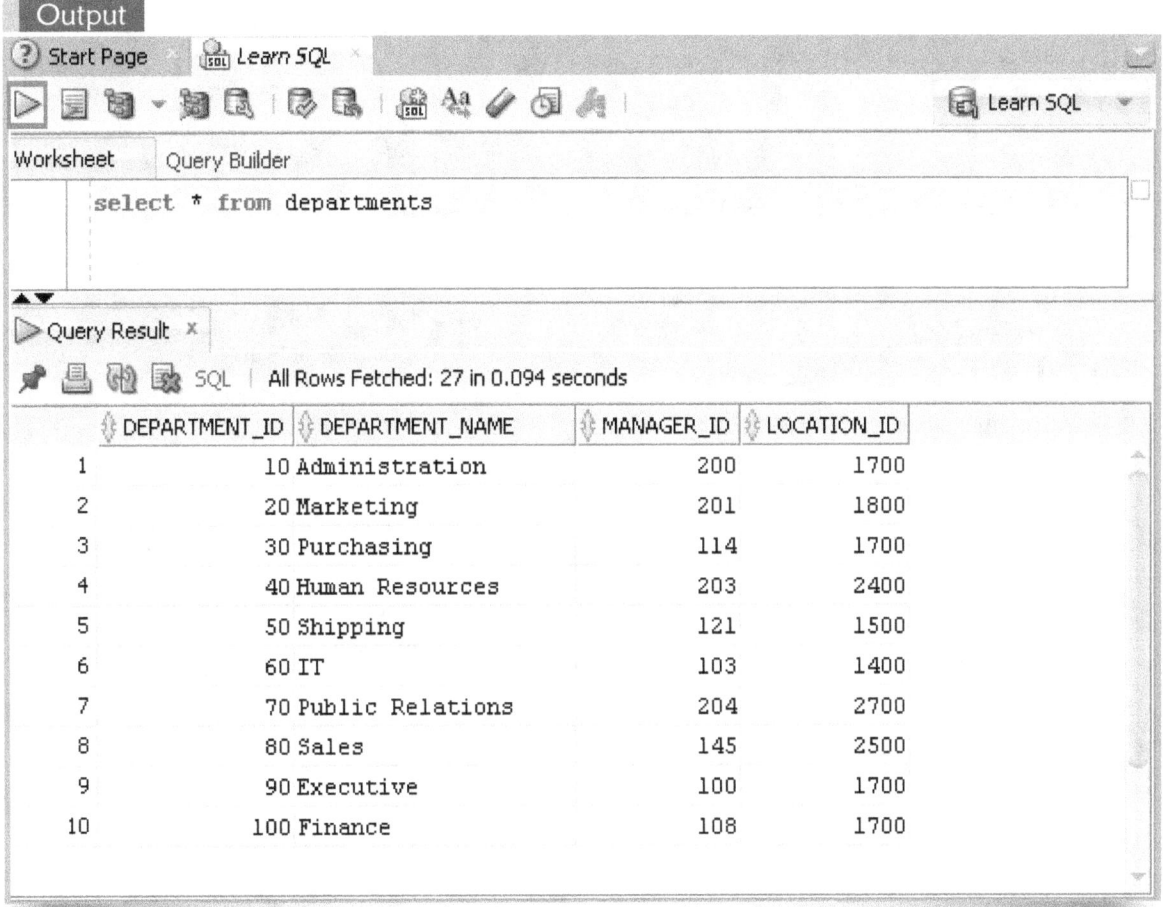

Chapter 3 – Retrieve Data From Database

Fetch Data from Selected Columns

The SELECT command also allows you to retrieve data from specific columns. By specifying the desired column names, separated by commas, you can restrict your query to display the result you wish to see. In the example present below, you restrict data from three columns (department number, last name of employee, and manager number) from the Employees table. Note that the result of your query displays columns in the same order as you specified them in the SELECT statement. Also note that all the three columns are separated by commas.

SQL Statement

SELECT   department_id, last_name, manager_id
FROM   employees;

Output

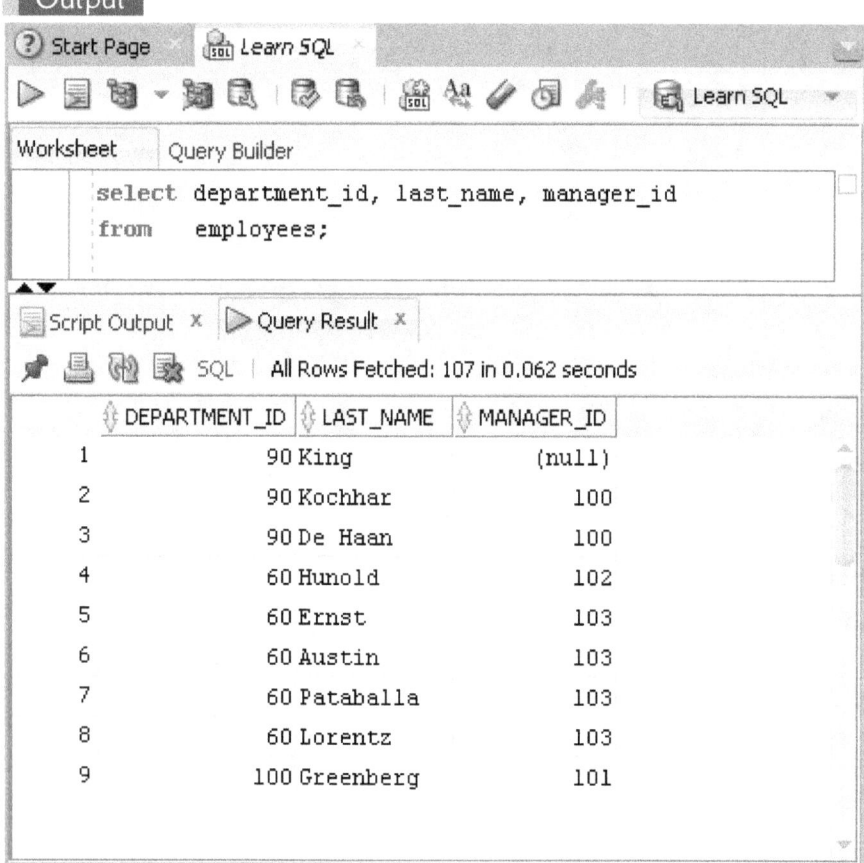

NOTE

In Oracle, you can use the DESCRIBE command to list columns in a table. For example, to see a list of all columns in the Employees table, you'll enter:

DESCRIBE Employees

Use the following commands to get table definitions in other DBMSs:

SQL Server:
sp_help 'employees'

DB2:
Describe table employees

MySQL:
Describe employees

MariaDB:
Show columns from employees;

PostgreSQL:
ld employees

SQLite:
Pragma table_info(employees);

Using Arithmetic Operators

You can create custom arithmetic expressions in your SELECT statement with the help of the common arithmetic operators defined in the table below. Besides SELECT, you are allowed to use these operators in any clause of a SQL statement except the FROM clause.

Operator	Description
+	Add
-	Subtract
*	Multiply
/	Divide

The following example uses the multiplication operator to display annual salary of all employees (by multiplying values in the table's salary column with a constant value i.e. 12) along with their commission percentages. Note that the resultant salary column (SALARY * 12) is not actually created in the Employees table, but is generated for display purpose only.

SQL Statement

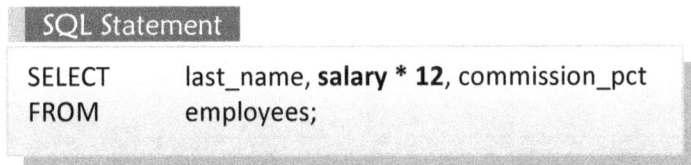

```
SELECT    last_name, salary * 12, commission_pct
FROM      employees;
```

Output

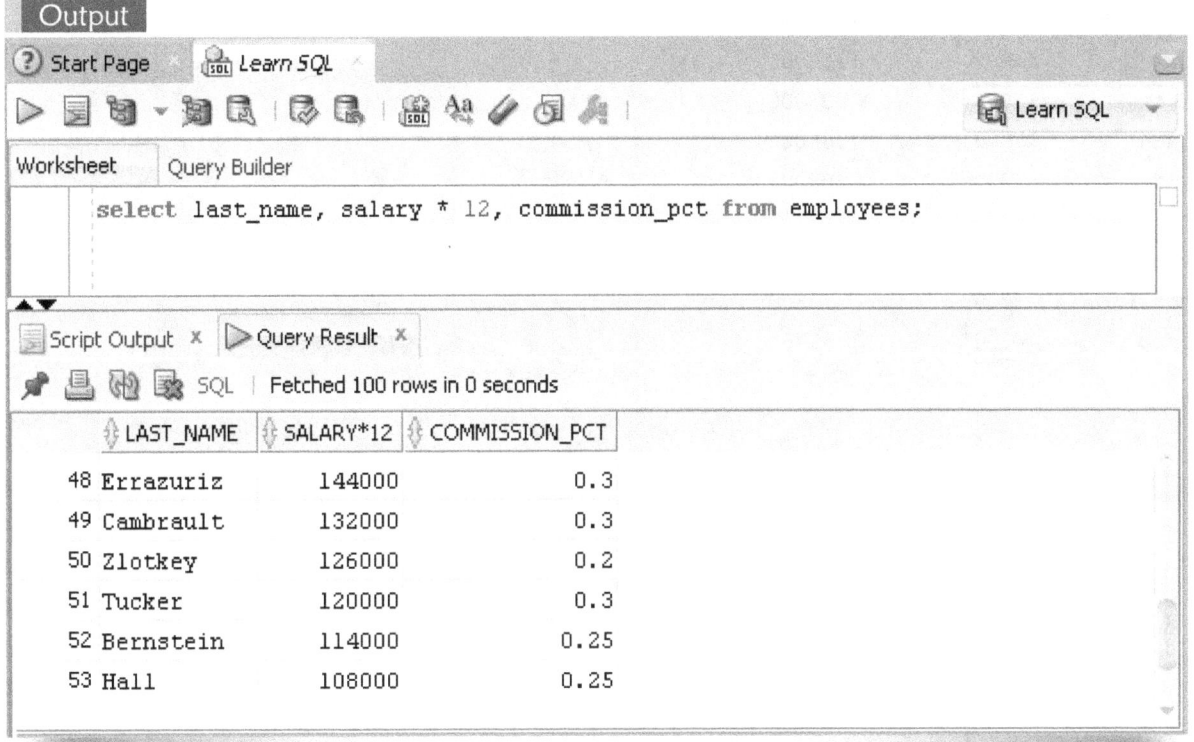

Arithmetic Operator Precedence

In the case of multiple arithmetic operators in a SQL statement, multiplication and division take precedence over addition and subtraction. If the operators are of the same priority, then they are evaluated from left to right. In the following example, the multiplication process is executed first and then the figure of 1000 is added to the result.

SQL Statement

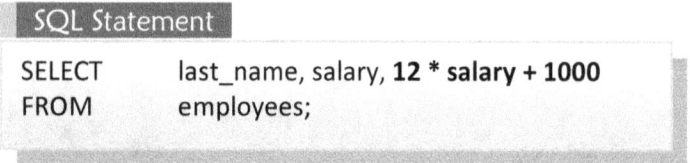

SELECT   last_name, salary, **12 * salary + 1000**
FROM   employees;

Output

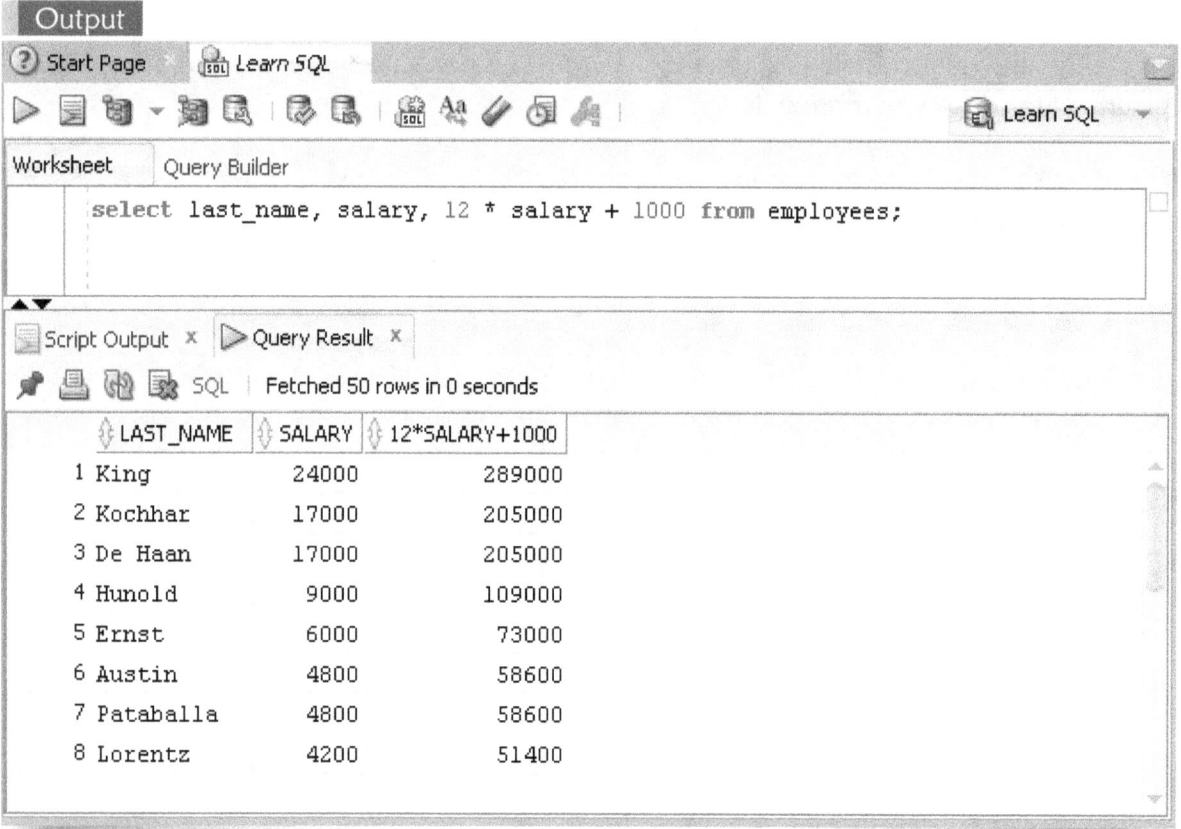

SQL for Everyone

Precedence with Parentheses

Parentheses are used to override the precedence rule. If you look at the previous example, the expression was executed in this order (for King): 12 * 24000 + 1000. In the current scenario, the result has changed because of the inclusion of the parentheses. In this case the expression is evaluated like this: (24000 + 1000) * 12.

SQL Statement

```
SELECT    last_name, salary, 12 * (salary + 1000)
FROM      employees;
```

Output

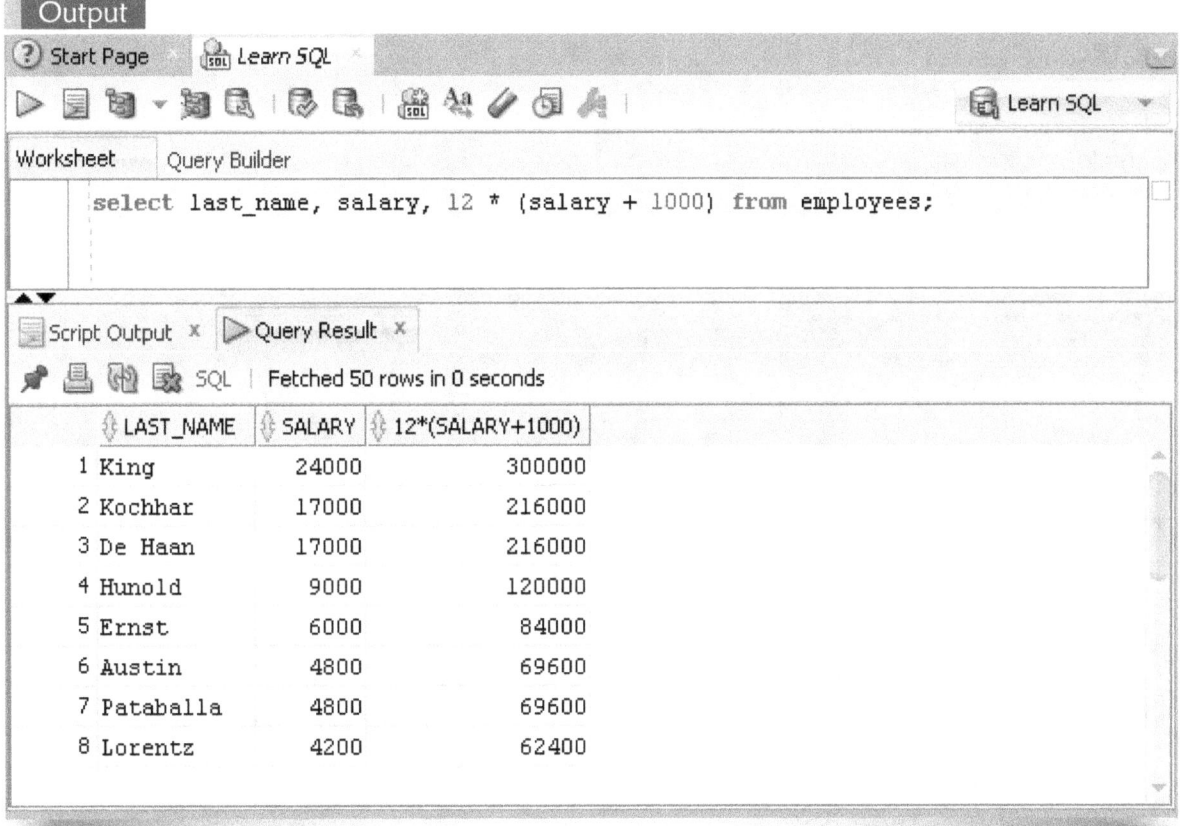

Change Column Headings

Usually when you query data from a table, the result is displayed with column names as the headings. Sometimes such headings are truncated and become difficult to understand. You encountered one such instance in the previous example, where you added an arithmetic expression to your query and the corresponding heading appeared as: 12 * (SALARY + 1000). You can change this heading into a meaningful title by using column alias clause. An alias is just an alternate name for a column. Add a column alias immediately after the column name (or expression), with a space between them. If an alias contains spaces, special characters (/ or #), or is case sensitive; it should be enclosed in double quotation marks. The AS keyword can also be included to comply ASNI SQL standards. The second statement uses a space between the two words and is therefore enclosed in double quotations.

SQL Statement

```
SELECT   last_name, salary, 12 * (salary + 1000) AS ANNUAL_SALARY
FROM     employees;

SELECT   last_name, salary, 12 * (salary + 1000) AS "Annual Salary"
FROM     employees;
```

Output

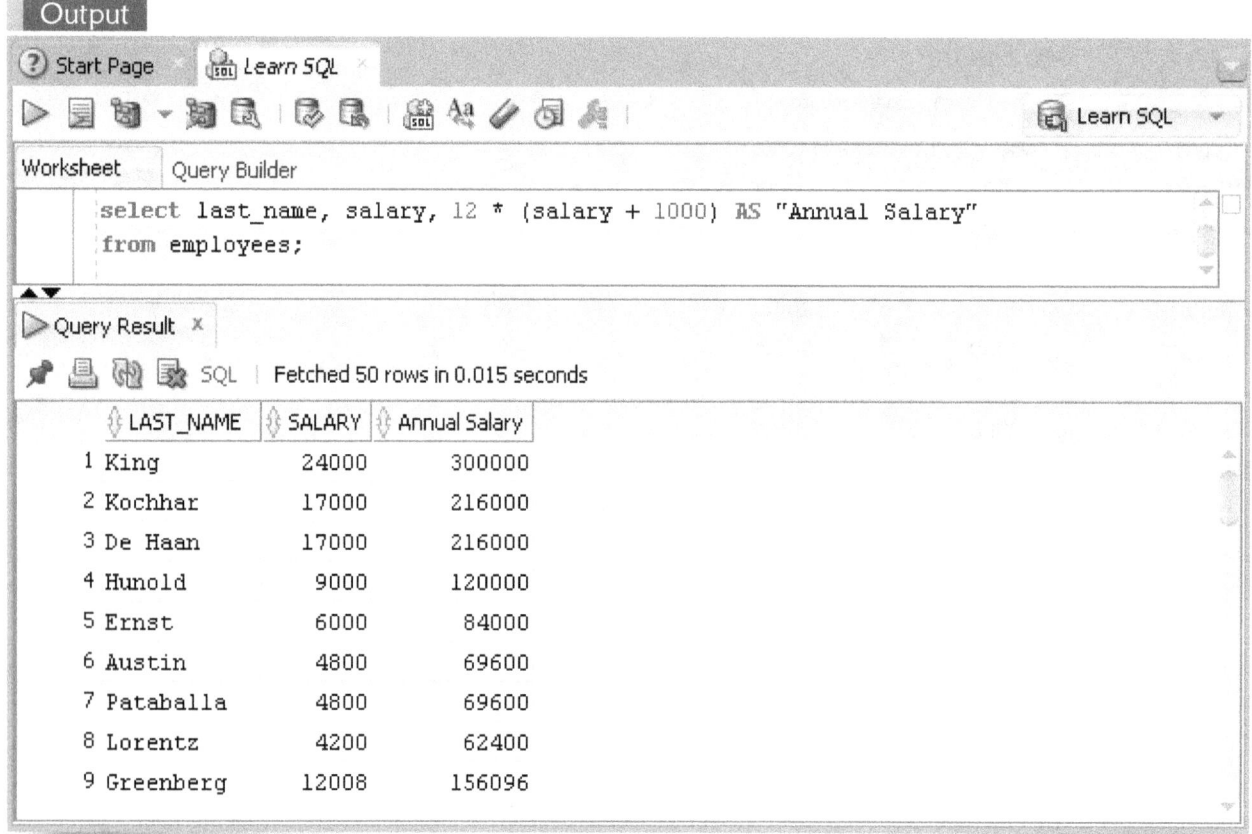

SQL for Everyone

Joining Columns

In your SELECT statement you can join two or more columns, arithmetic expressions, or constant values into a single column using the concatenation operator which is represented by two vertical bars (||). The resultant column is generated as a character expression. In the following example, we combined first and last names of employees and presented the values under a new title: Employees.

SQL Statement

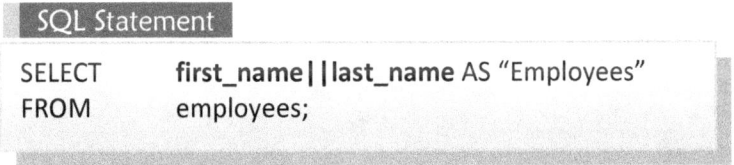

```
SELECT      first_name||last_name AS "Employees"
FROM        employees;
```

Output

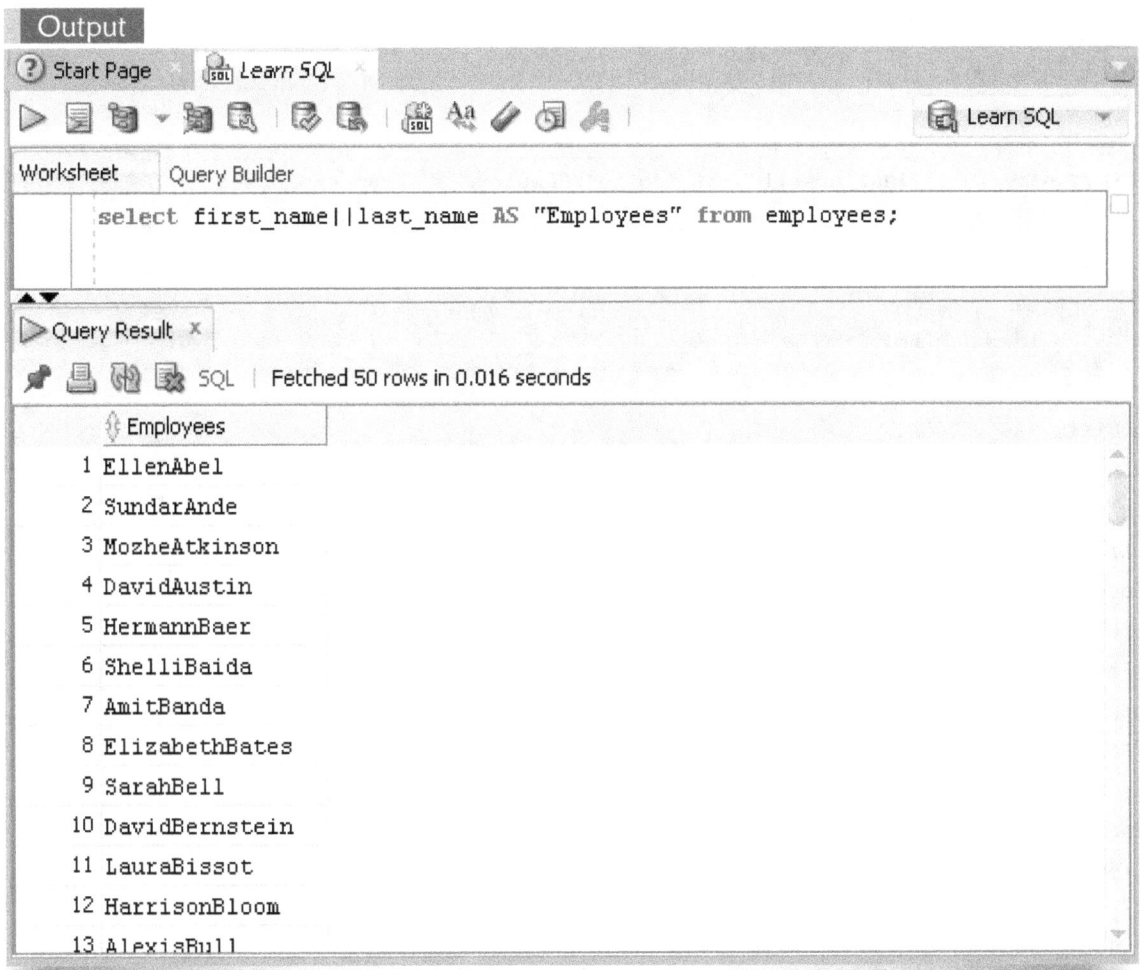

Joining Columns (continued)

In the following example, you added a couple of constant values to your SELECT statement for better readability. First, you added a space between the two names with the help of a space character – represented by two single quotes having a single space between them. Secondly, you added a comma (also enclosed in single quotes) to separate the name of an employee from his/her job id.

SQL Statement

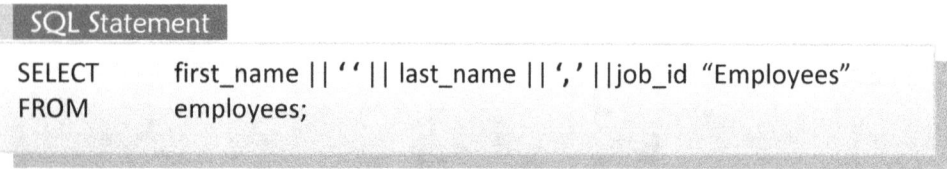

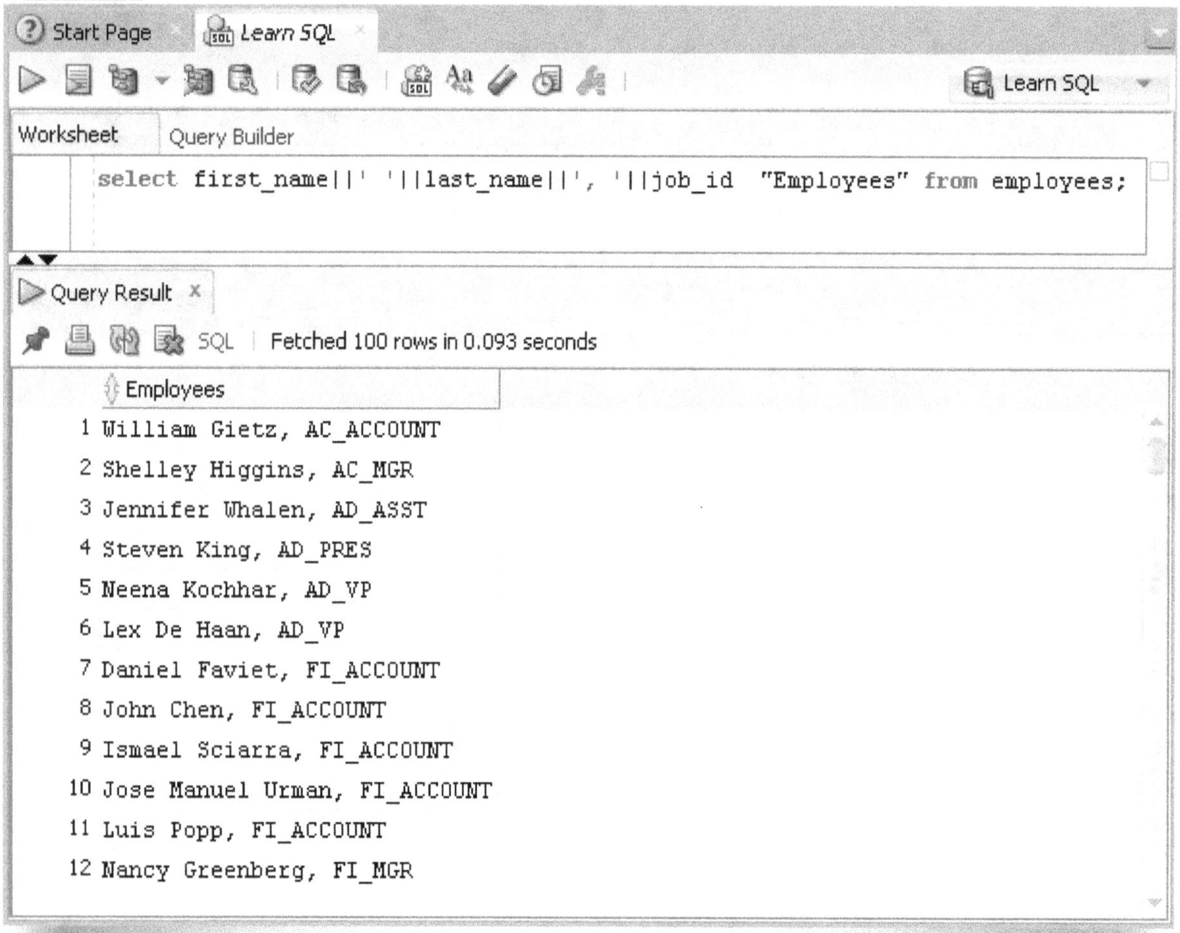

```
SELECT      first_name || ' ' || last_name || ',' ||job_id  "Employees"
FROM        employees;
```

Output

Start Page
Learn SQL
Learn SQL
Worksheet
Query Builder
select first_name||' '||last_name||', '||job_id "Employees" from employees;
Query Result
SQL
Fetched 100 rows in 0.093 seconds
Employees
1 William Gietz, AC_ACCOUNT
2 Shelley Higgins, AC_MGR
3 Jennifer Whalen, AD_ASST
4 Steven King, AD_PRES
5 Neena Kochhar, AD_VP
6 Lex De Haan, AD_VP
7 Daniel Faviet, FI_ACCOUNT
8 John Chen, FI_ACCOUNT
9 Ismael Sciarra, FI_ACCOUNT
10 Jose Manuel Urman, FI_ACCOUNT
11 Luis Popp, FI_ACCOUNT
12 Nancy Greenberg, FI_MGR

NOTE

- Access and SQL Server use + for concatenation.
- Oracle, DB2, SQLite, and PostgreSQL support | |.
- MySQL and MariaDB provide Concat() function for this purpose.

NULL Values

If a table column lacks a value in it, that value is said to be NULL. Zeros or spaces cannot be defined as NULL values, because zero is a number, and a space is a character. A null value can be defined as: **A value that is inapplicable, unavailable, unknown, or unassigned**. If you look at the COMMISSION_PCT column's data in the Employees table, you'll notice that employees other than sales personnel have null values in this column and this is because the commission percentage is **inapplicable** to these employees.

The following example calculates a null commission for employees who have no commission percentage (null) mentioned against their names. Salaries multiplied with NULL commission percentages resulted in null commission values.

SQL Statement

```
SELECT    last_name, job_id, salary, commission_pct, salary * commission_pct/100 "Commission"
FROM      employees;
```

Output

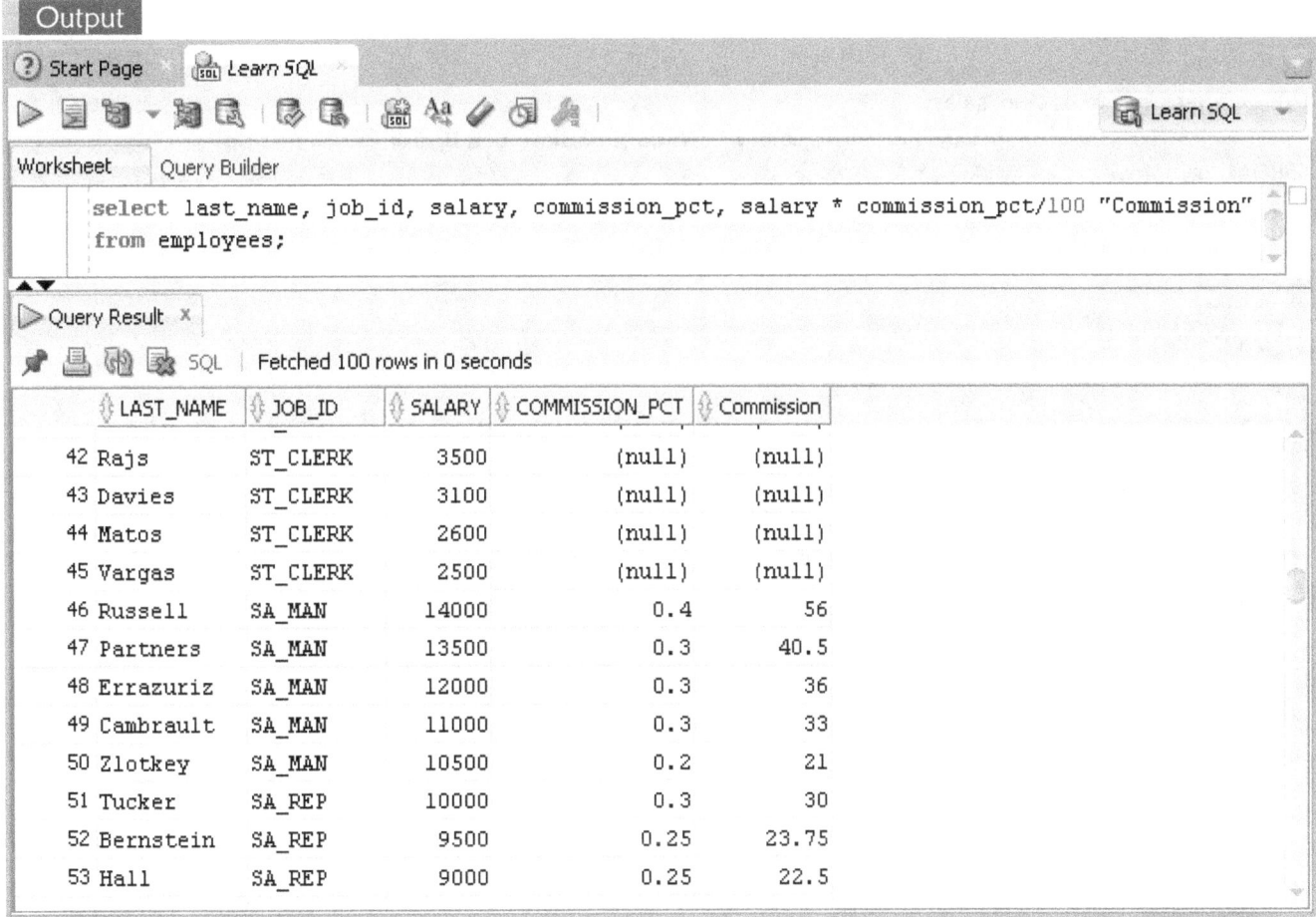

Chapter 3 – Retrieve Data From Database

Replacing NULL Values Using NVL Function

In the previous example, you saw that null values in the calculated commission column displayed (null) for employees other than sales representatives, which is not considered a good presentation of data. To override this default value with some acceptable text, you are provided with NVL function. Before we see a practical example, let's first acquaint ourselves with its syntax:

Syntax

NVL(expression1, expression 2)

According to the syntax, you put source column or expression containing null in expression1 position, and the target value that you wish to see instead of null is placed in expression2. NVL function can be used to convert any data type. One thing that you have to take care of is the use of expression2 which must be of same data type as that of expression1. For example, if you're converting a numeric column, then you must use a number in expression2 position. Repeating the previous example, you'll add the NVL function to convert null values – in COMMISSION_PCT (a table column) and COMMISSION (an arithmetic expression) – to zero in the following SQL statement.

SQL Statement

```
SELECT  last_name, job_id, salary,
        nvl(commission_pct,0) "Percent",  salary * nvl(commission_pct, 0)/100 "Commission"
FROM    employees;
```

Output

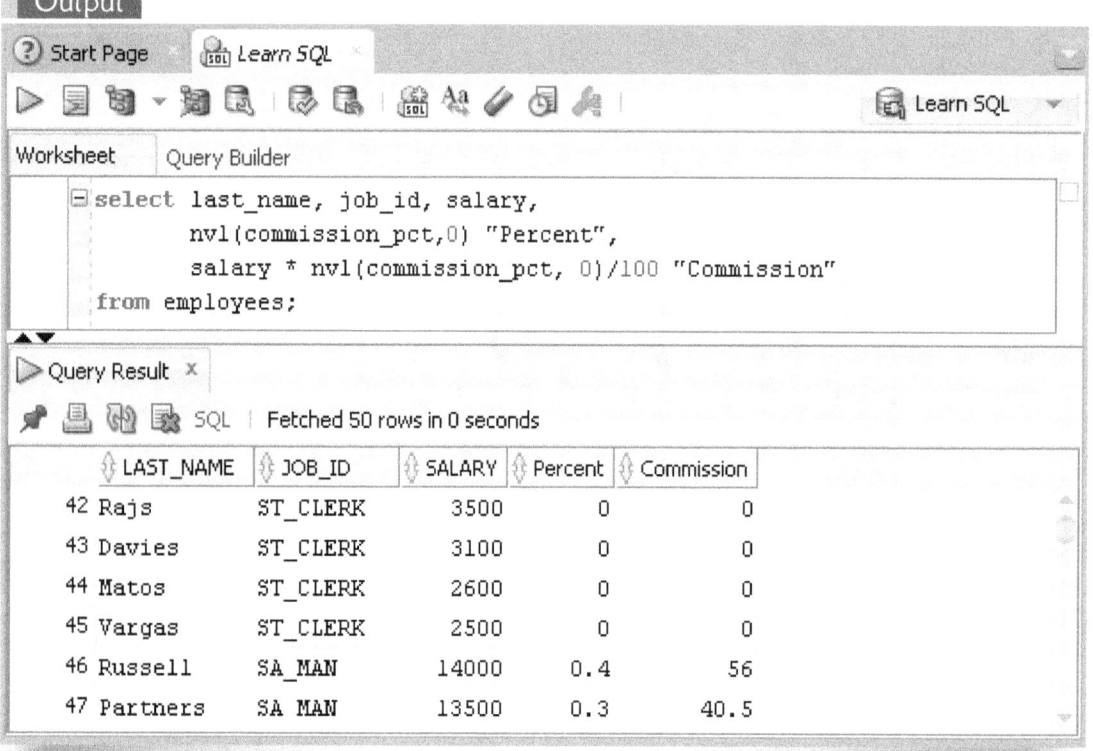

SQL for Everyone

Preventing Duplicates with DISTINCT

By default, a SELECT statement returns result of a query without eliminating duplicate records. For instance, if you execute **select job_id from employees**, you will get all records including some duplicate entries in the job_id column. In order to fetch unique job ids, you will have to use the DISTINCT clause just after the SELECT keyword, as shown in the following example.

SQL Statement

```
SELECT    distinct job_id
FROM      employees;
```

Output

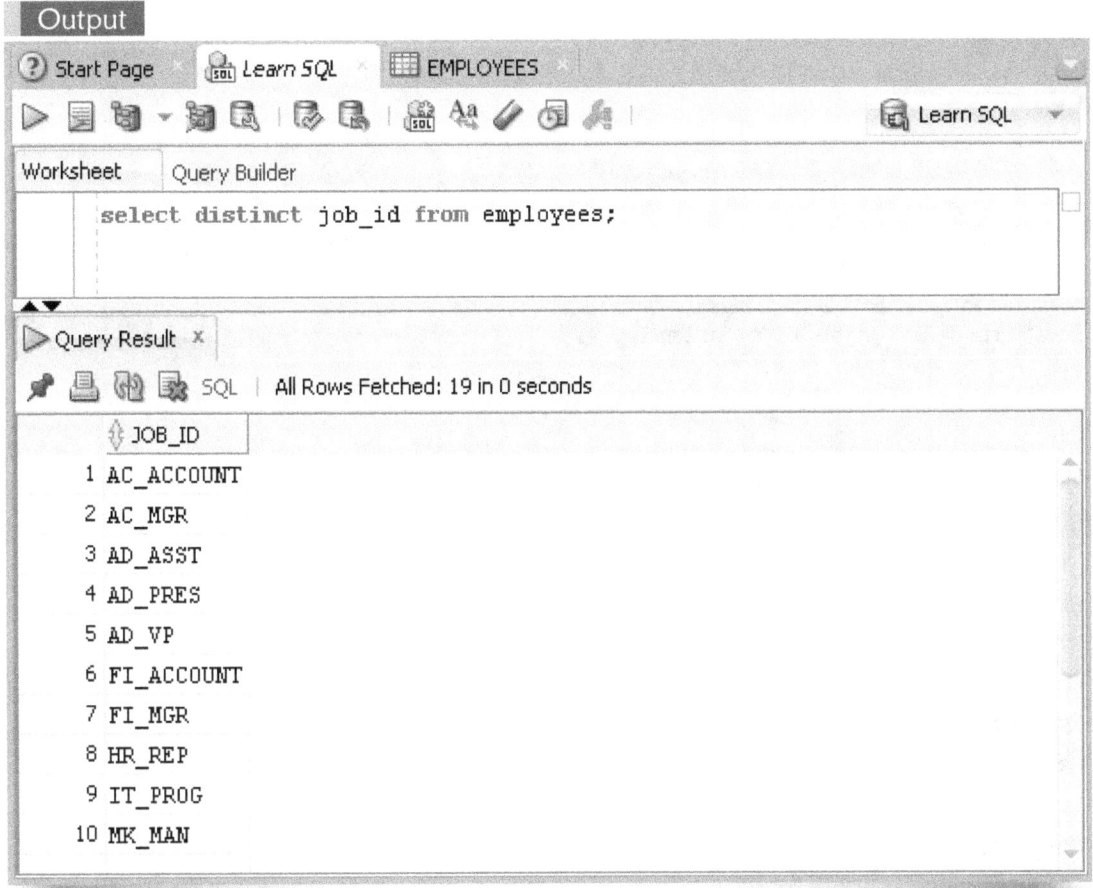

Multiple Distinct Columns

In the previous example, you used just one column (JOB_ID) to display unique values. DISTINCT can also be applied to all the columns in a SELECT statement. With DISTINCT applied to multiple columns, the returned dataset displays distinct combination of the selected columns as shown in the following example, which shows all the different combinations of FIRST_NAME and JOB_ID. Since there are no two employees with the same first name and the same job id, the query fetches all rows from the table. If, for instance, there were two employees having Alexander as their first name enrolled under the job id IT_PROG, the result would have shown just one record.

SQL Statement

```
SELECT      distinct first_name, job_id
FROM        employees;
```

Output

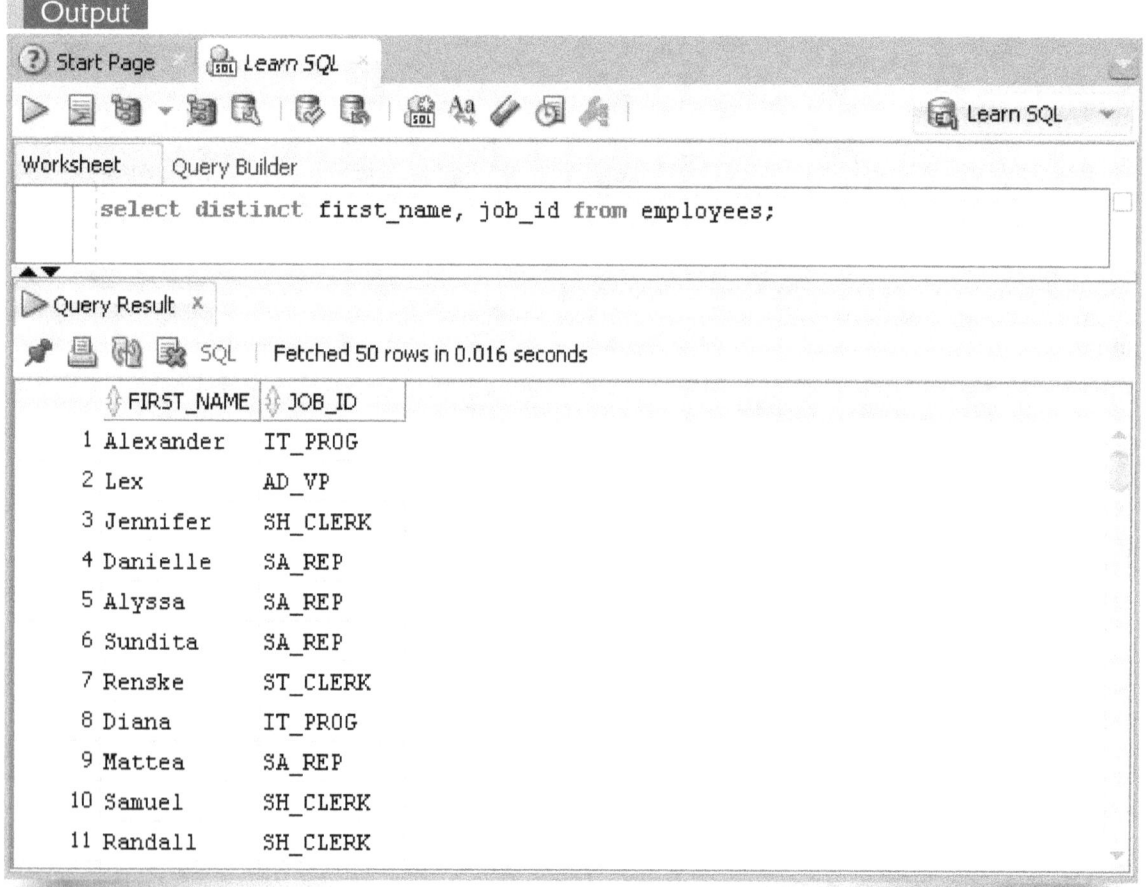

SQL for Everyone

Sorting Records

In all the previous examples you retrieved data without specifying any specific sort order. To sort the fetched data in some desired order, you use the ORDER BY clause. By default this clause sorts data in ascending order. You can use the DESC option to have the output in descending order. If used, this clause must be placed last in the SELECT statement. The following query is sorted on the last name of employees. Another alternate is to specify the position of the columns you wish to sort data on. For instance, rather than entering the column name (LAST_NAME), you can use its position like this: ORDER BY 1. Moreover, you can add as many columns to the ORDER BY clause as there are number of columns in a table. To sort by multiple columns, simply specify the column names separated by commas (just as you do when you are selecting multiple columns). For example, if you are displaying an employee list, you might want to display it sorted by last name and first name (first by last name, and then within each last name sort by first name).

SQL Statement

```
SELECT    last_name, department_id, hire_date
FROM      employees
ORDER BY  last_name;
```

> **NOTE**
> It is legal to sort the output by a column that is not retrieved in your query. In the case of multiple columns, the output is displayed exactly in the order of the sort sequence specified. For example, if you sort the query by last name and department id, the result will be sorted first by the last name and then by the department id.

Output

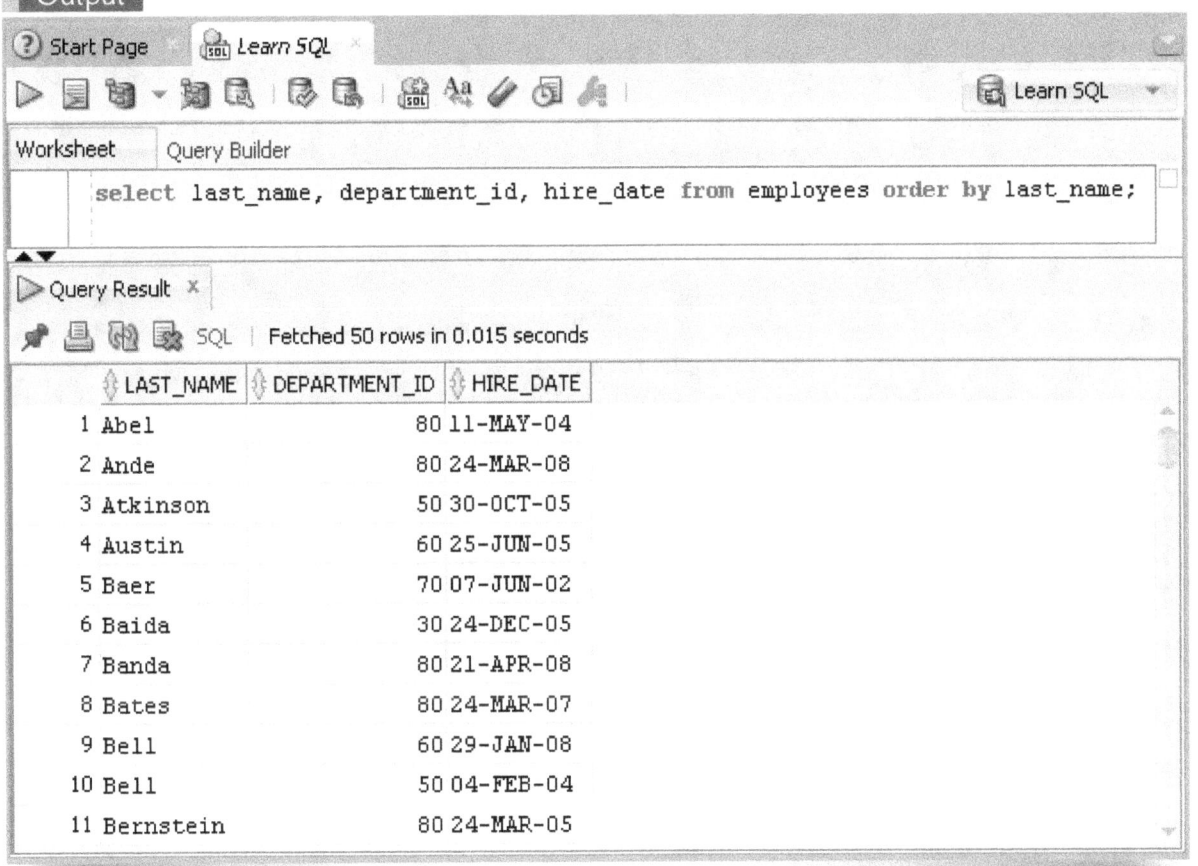

Chapter 3 – Retrieve Data From Database

Comparison and Logical Operators with Precedence Rules

Comparison and logical operators are used in the WHERE clause of a SQL statement (the WHERE clause is discussed in the next section). These operators assist in evaluating some conditions to fetch desired dataset. Suppose that you have a table named Contact having three records as shown in the following figure.

These records are used in the "Example" column below to provide an overview about the comparison and logical operators that will be used thoroughly in upcoming exercises.

```
+----+---------------+------------------------+------+--------------------+
| id | name          | email                  | age  | message            |
+----+---------------+------------------------+------+--------------------+
|  1 | Riaz Ahmed    | realtech@cyber.net.pk  |   30 | Feedback message   |
|  2 | Daniel Clarke | daniel@gmail.com       |   25 | This is a comment  |
| 99 | NULL          | abc@abc.com            | NULL | This is a message  |
+----+---------------+------------------------+------+--------------------+
```

Comparison Operators

Operator	Description	Example
=	Equal to	SELECT * FROM Contact where Name = 'Riaz Ahmed'; *Returns record # 1*
<> or != or ^=	Not Equal to	SELECT * FROM Contact where Name <> 'Riaz Ahmed'; *Returns record # 2*
>	Greater than	SELECT * FROM Contact where Age > 25; *Returns record # 1*
>=	Greater than or equal	SELECT * FROM Contact where Age >= 25; *Returns record # 1 and 2*
<	Less than	SELECT * FROM Contact where Id < 2; *Returns record # 1*
<=	Less than or equal	SELECT * FROM Contact where Id <= 2; *Returns record # 1 and 2*
BETWEEN ... AND ...	Data range between two values	SELECT * FROM Contact where Id **BETWEEN 2 AND 100**; *Returns record # 2and 99*
LIKE	Matches a pattern	SELECT * FROM Contact where message **LIKE** '%feed%'; *Returns record # 1*
IN	Search multiple values	SELECT * FROM Contact where name **IN** ('Riaz Ahmed', 'Daniel Clarke'); *Returns record # 1 and 2*
IS NULL	Fetches null values	SELECT * FROM Contact where name **IS NULL** *Returns record # 3*

Logical Operators

Operator	Description	Example
AND	Both conditions must evaluate to true	SELECT * FROM Contact where name='Riaz Ahmed' **AND** age=30; *Returns record # 1*
OR	Either condition returns true	SELECT * FROM Contact where name='Riaz Ahmed' **OR** age=25; *Returns record # 1 and 2*
NOT	Evaluates the opposite condition	SELECT * FROM Contact where name **IS NOT NULL** *Returns record # 1 and 2*
AND OR combined	Can be used in the same logical expression	SELECT * FROM Contact where name='Riaz Ahmed' **AND** (age=25 **OR** age=30 **OR** age=99); *Returns record # 1*

> **NOTE**
>
> When used in conjunction with the four SQL operators (and with the arithmetic operator), the NOT logical operator produces negating results. For instance, if you add the NOT operator to the above examples as follows, you will get opposing records.
>
> **NOT Name = 'Riaz Ahmed'**
> **NOT BETWEEN 2 AND 100**
> **NOT LIKE '%feed%'**
> **NOT IN ('Riaz Ahmed', 'Daniel Clarke')**
> **name IS NOT NULL**
>
> *If the value being compared is a character string, (for example, Riaz Ahmed), or a date, then enclose it under single quotation marks; numbers should be entered without quotes.*
>
> In MariaDB, you can use the NOT operator to negate BETWEEN, IN, and EXISTS clauses as compared to other DBMS where it can be used to negate any conditions.

Precedence Rules for Comparison and Logical Operators

Comparison and logical operators also follow some precedence rules as followed by the arithmetic operators. The following table lists the evaluation order for these operators.

Evaluation Order	Operators
1	All comparison Operators (=, <>, >, >=, <, <=, BETWEEN, LIKE, IN, IS NULL)
2	AND
3	OR

- Comparison operators are evaluated first, even in negating expressions.
- AND has a higher precedence over OR.
- Equal precedence operators are evaluated from left to right.

Similar to the arithmetic operators, precedence for these operators can also be overridden by placing part of an expression in parentheses. Expression enclosed in parentheses are evaluated first, as demonstrated in the last example in the Logical Operators section above.

Filtering Data with the WHERE Clause

All the SELECT statements used in the previous examples were issued to retrieve all rows (records) from the defined tables. To limit the number of returned rows from the query, you use the WHERE clause which should be used immediately after the FROM clause. In this clause you specify a condition comprising three components: expression, comparison operator, and value.

Syntax

... WHERE *expression comparison operator value*

Here, *expression* can be a table column, a constant value, or an expression itself. A condition is evaluated by comparing the data defined in the **expression** position with the **value** using the **comparison operator**. In subsequent exercises you will go through different flavors of the WHERE clause. But here, you are provided with couple of simple examples to show some basic usage of this clause.

In the first statement below, LOCATION_ID (a column name) performs as an *expression*, (=) is the *comparison operator*, and 1700 is the *value* which is being compared with the expression. The query retrieves all records (with all columns - *) for the departments established under location number 1700.

In the second example, we used the BETWEEN operator and specified a range of values to get a list of employees who are earning between 100 and 10000.

SQL Statements

```
SELECT      *
FROM        departments
WHERE       location_id = 1700;
```

```
SELECT      *
FROM        employees
WHERE       salary between 100 and 10000
ORDER BY    salary;
```

Comparing Character Strings in the WHERE Clause

To compare a character string in a WHERE clause, you have to enclose the string in single quotation marks (' '). The following example searches an employee whose first name is JOHN. When you execute the statement, no rows will be returned, because character strings are case sensitive and should be entered according to the data stored in the table. Since the first name of the searched employee is saved as *John* in the database, changing the character string from JOHN to John will fetch the match, as shown in the output screenshot.

Alternatively, you can use the UPPER built-in function to match the provided value, like this: WHERE UPPER(first_name)='JOHN'. In this condition, the UPPER function is used to first convert the column value to upper case before matching it with the provided value. This function is discussed on page 53.

SQL Statement

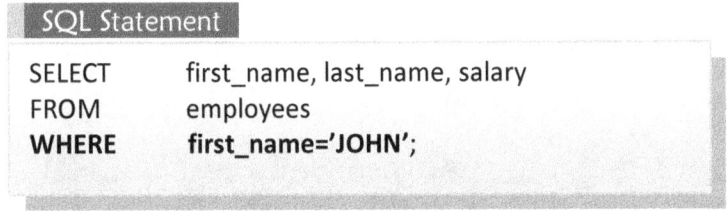

```
SELECT    first_name, last_name, salary
FROM      employees
WHERE     first_name='JOHN';
```

Output

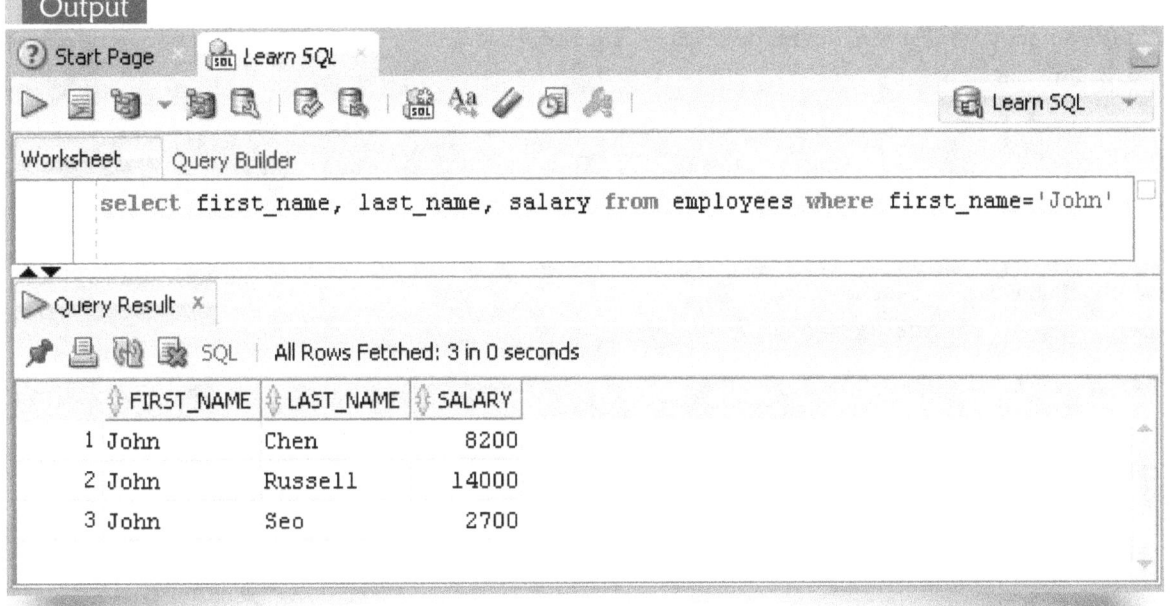

The BETWEEN Operator

The BETWEEN operator is used in situations where you are searching records between, and inclusive of, a range. You provide a lower value just after the BETWEEN keyword, and put the higher value after the AND logical operator as demonstrated in the following example, where you are trying to fetch employees records whose join date is between 01-JAN-06 and 31-JAN-06, inclusive. Note that date values are also enclosed in single quotation marks and are defined in the default format as 'DD-MON-YY'. See Page 57 for further details on changing default date formats.

SQL Statement

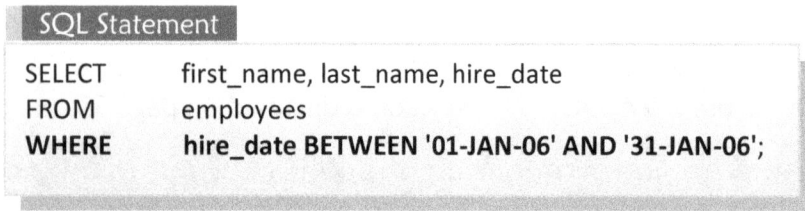

```
SELECT     first_name, last_name, hire_date
FROM       employees
WHERE      hire_date BETWEEN '01-JAN-06' AND '31-JAN-06';
```

Output

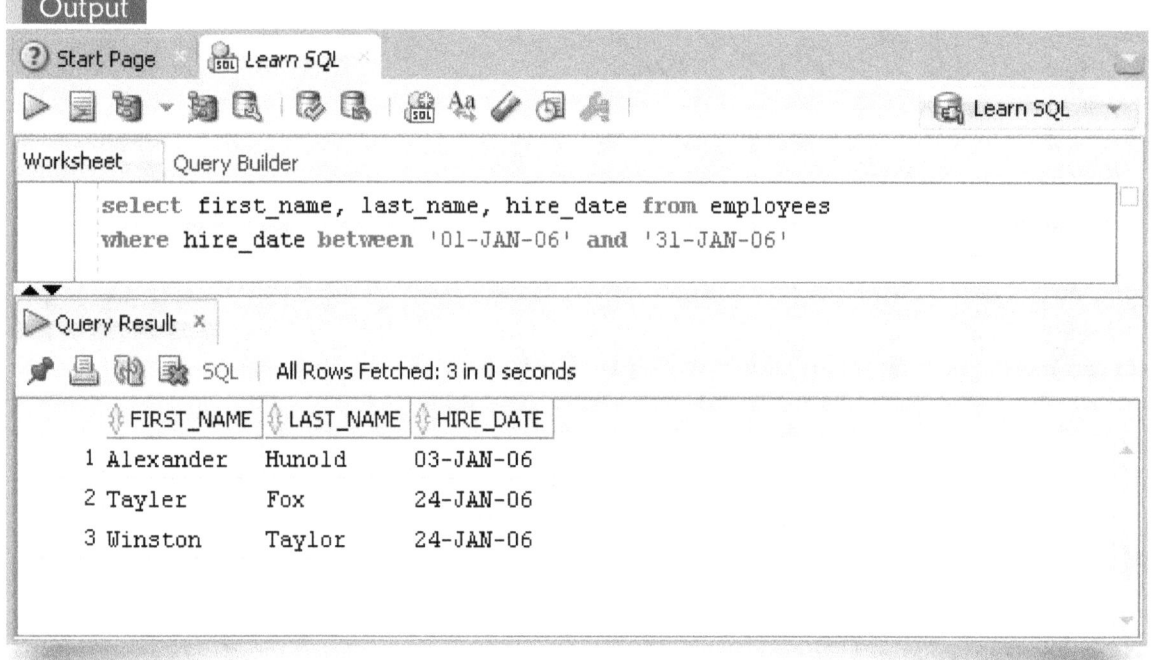

SQL for Everyone

The IN Operator

Suppose, you wish to see a list of departments under two different locations i.e. 1800 and 2700. If you use the BETWEEN operator, you'll get a list of departments (including those falling between the two ranges) that you don't intend to see. Another alternate will be to use a list of conditions like: location_id=1800 OR location_id=2700. Although it is a valid condition, but what if you add ten or more locations to your WHERE clause? Obviously, the statement will grow up in size and you won't like typing such long statements that consequently enhances program code. To cope with the situation, you're provided with the IN operator, where you just provide a list of desired values in parentheses, as shown in the following example. Since location_id is a numeric field, you provided the values without the quotation marks. Note that only characters and dates used in the IN list are enclosed within single quotes.

SQL Statement

```
SELECT     department_id, department_name, location_id
FROM       departments
WHERE      location_id IN (1800,2700);
```

> **NOTE**
> The use of the IN operator is a cleaner way if you are working with long lists of conditions. Secondly, the IN operator can also contain another SELECT statement to form a more dynamic WHERE clause.

Output

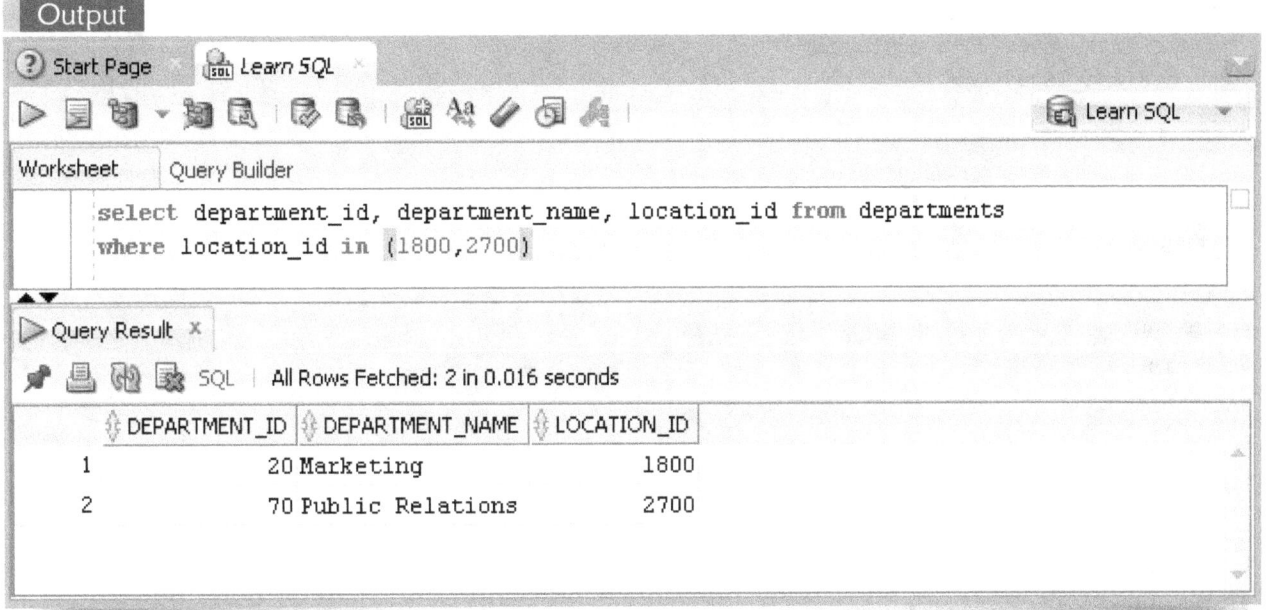

35

The LIKE Operator

In many situations you search for records in your database whose exact values are unknown. Using the LIKE operator along with a character pattern (search string) you can easily find the match. The character pattern is constructed with the help of two special characters: % and _. The percent character (%) represents zero or more characters, while the underscore character (_) represents just one. The first example below searches all employees starting with the letter 'A'. The second statement displays a list of all employees who do not contain 'a' within their names. The third example searches for employees whose first name has an 'a' as the second letter.

SQL Statement

```
SELECT     first_name
FROM       employees
WHERE      first_name LIKE 'A%';
```

NOTE:
Some DBMS are case sensitive, therefore you must take care of it while using the LIKE operator. For example, such DBMS would treat 'adam' and 'Adam' differently.

Microsoft Access uses * instead of % and ? instead of _.

Output

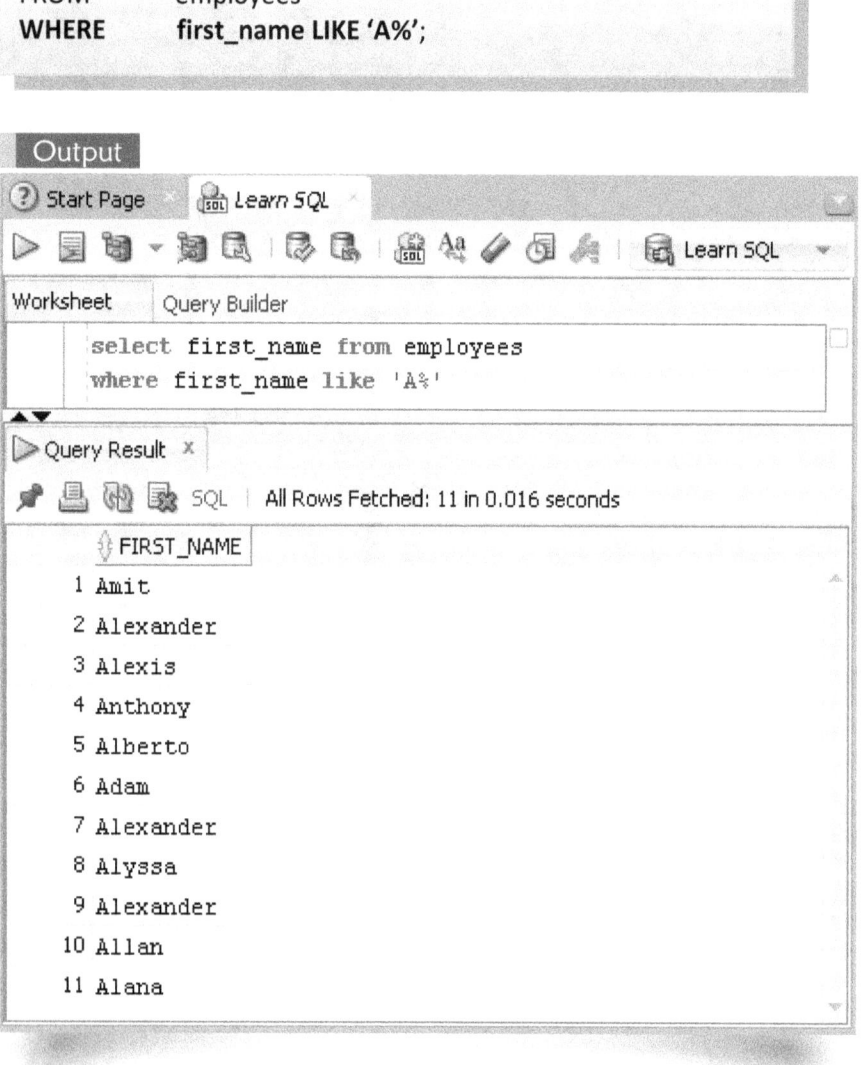

SQL Statement

```
SELECT     first_name
FROM       employees
WHERE      first_name NOT LIKE '%a%';
```

Output

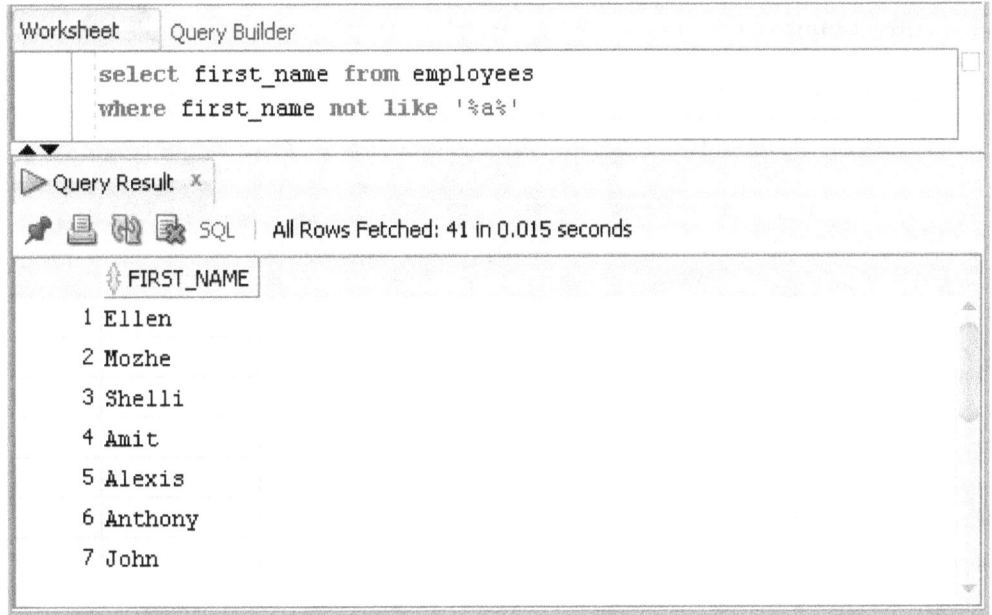

SQL Statement

```
SELECT     first_name
FROM       employees
WHERE      first_name LIKE '_a%';
```

Output

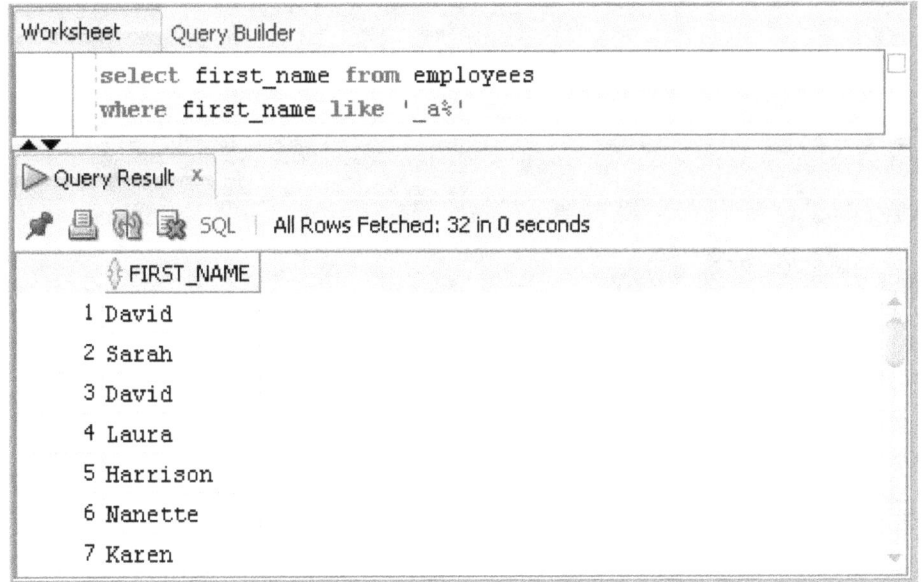

The IS NULL Operator

A null value, as mentioned earlier, is a value that is unavailable or inapplicable. It is neither said to be a zero nor can it be represented as a space. Also, you cannot use an equal to operator (=) in the WHERE clause to match null values. The valid procedure to find a null match is to use the IS NULL operator. In the first two examples below you won't get any record. In the first statement the equal to (=) comparison operator is used, and in the second one, the statement is tried with an empty space (' '). In fact, the second query will also throw an "invalid number" error, because you are comparing a numeric column with an empty string. The third query is correct which uses the IS NULL operator to display records of sales representatives. To get negating records (other than sales personnel), use the NOT logical operator in the WHERE clause like this: commission_pct IS NOT NULL.

SQL Statements

```
SELECT    first_name, last_name, commission_pct
FROM      employees
WHERE     commission_pct=NULL;
```

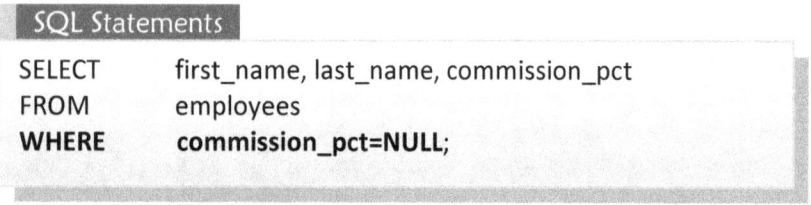

```
SELECT    first_name, last_name, commission_pct
FROM      employees
WHERE     commission_pct=' ';
```

```
SELECT    first_name, last_name, commission_pct
FROM      employees
WHERE     commission_pct IS NULL;
```

Output

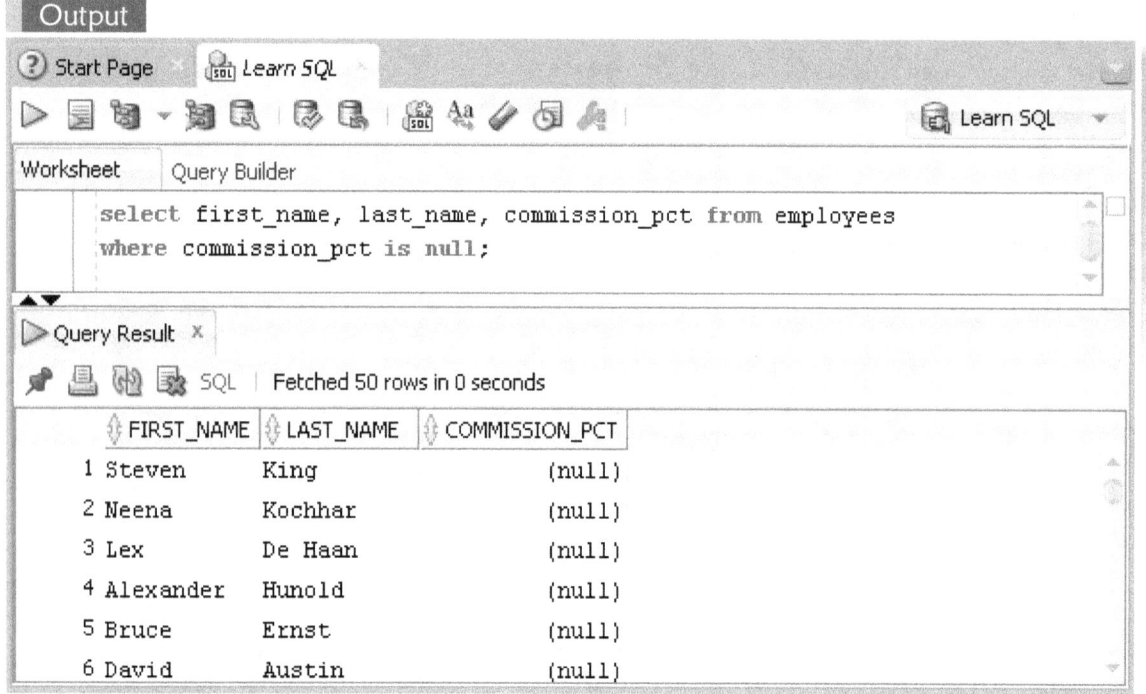

AND/OR Operators

Always remember the following rules for the AND and OR logical operators:

- AND will return rows only when both conditions are TRUE.
- OR requires either condition to be TRUE.
- AND has a higher precedence over OR.

Note that both these operators can be used together in the WHERE clause of a SQL statement to construct compound logical expression.

The WHERE clause in the following example is made up of two conditions, and the keyword AND is used to join them. AND instructs the database management system software to return only rows that meet all the conditions specified. If a record has department number 20, but the job id is not MK_MAN (Marketing Manager), it is not retrieved. Similarly, records having job id MK_MAN in other departments will not to be retrieved as well.

In the first example below, the AND operator is used to search employees working in department number 20 as MK_MAN. As you can see, the sole fetched record fulfills both conditions - mentioned before and after the AND operator. The example contains a single AND clause and is thus made up of two filter conditions. To narrow the result, you are allowed to add more filter conditions, each separated by an AND keyword like this: WHERE department_id=20 **AND** job_id='MK_MAN' **AND** first_name='Michael'

SQL Statement

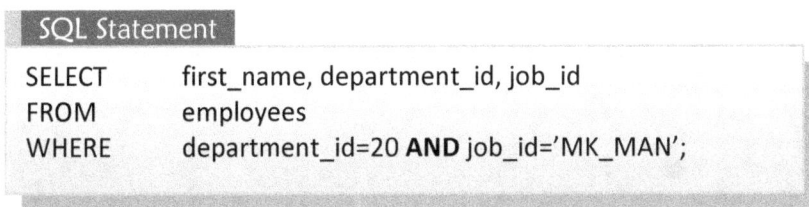

```
SELECT    first_name, department_id, job_id
FROM      employees
WHERE     department_id=20 AND job_id='MK_MAN';
```

Output

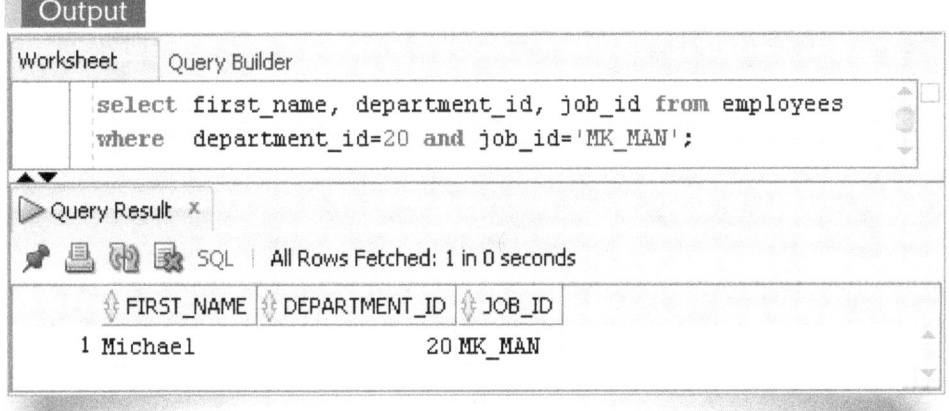

The second logical operator that you can use in you SQL statement is the OR operator which is less restrictive and thus returns more rows. Most database management systems do not even evaluate the second condition in an OR WHERE clause if the first condition has already been met i.e. the rows are returned without considering the second condition if the first condition evaluates to true.

The query mentioned below, fetches all employees who are either in department number 20 OR who work as MK_MAN. The second record returned by the query doesn't fulfills the job id part of the condition, but since it satisfies the first condition (department_id =20), it is picked by the query for display.

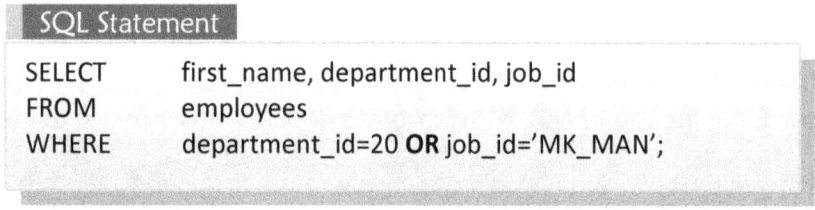

SQL Statement	
SELECT	first_name, department_id, job_id
FROM	employees
WHERE	department_id=20 **OR** job_id='MK_MAN';

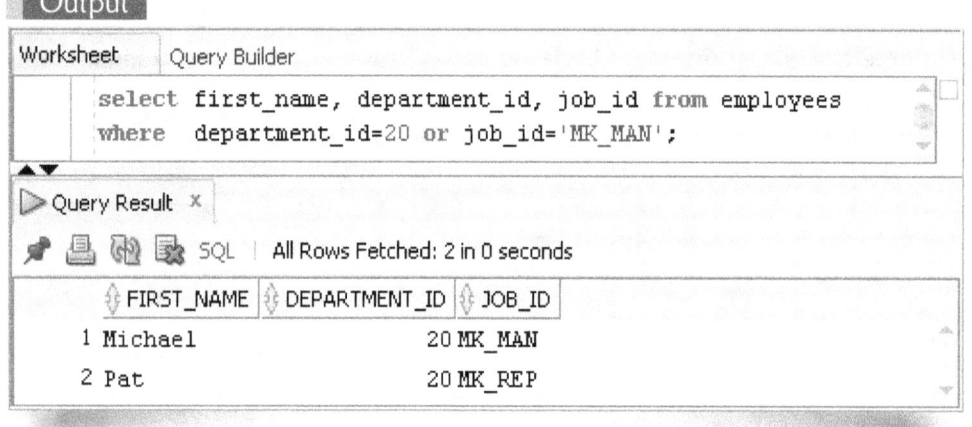

AND/OR Used Together

You can use any number of AND and OR operators together in a single WHERE clause to create complex filtering. But, putting these two together in a WHERE clause may also put you in trouble. Let's see an example of this. You are asked to provide a list of all employees working either in department number 10 or 20 and are earning more than or equal to 6000. In response, you created a query like this:

```
Select  first_name||' '||last_name Employee, department_id, salary
from    employees
where   department_id=10 or department_id=20 and salary >= 6000
```

Output

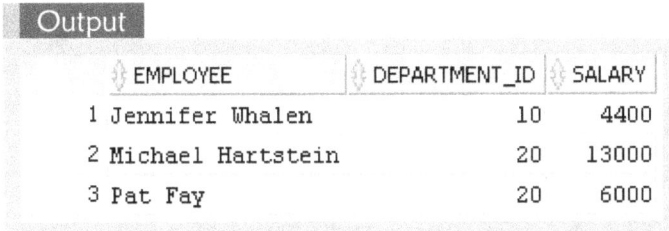

Look at the record of Jennifer Whalen. This should have been filtered out (because of the AND condition which says that the salary must be greater than or equal to 6000). Why this record appeared? The answer is the order of evaluation. As mentioned earlier, AND operator has higher precedence over OR, therefore the WHERE clause in the above statement was executed in the following order:

1. department_id = 20 and salary >= 6000 - returned second and third records.
2. department_id = 10 - returned record number 1 of Jennifer Whalen.

This happened because of the precedence rule that joined wrong operators together. Again, the solution to the problem lies in the use of parentheses to explicitly group related operators. Modify the statement by enclosing the first two filters within parentheses, as shown below.

```
Select  first_name||' '||last_name Employee, department_id, salary
from    employees
where   (department_id=10 or department_id=20) and salary >= 6000
```

Output

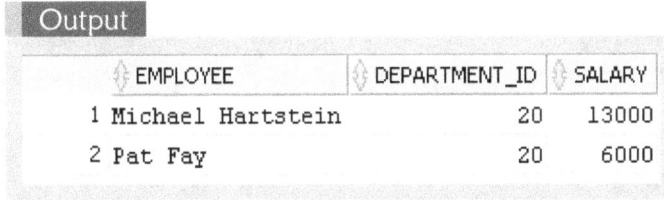

Since parentheses have a higher order of evaluation than either AND or OR operators, the OR condition (within the parentheses) was evaluated first like this:

1. (department_id=10 or department_id=20)
2. salary >= 6000

Now, the statement fetches records of employees working under department number 10 or department number 20 earning 6000 or more. Although Jennifer is working in department number 10, she doesn't meet the second criterion and is thus filtered out.

Chapter 3 – Retrieve Data From Database

Add Comments to SQL Statements

So far, you've been using very simple SQL statements to fetch the desired information from your DBMS. Once you become a guru, you start writing lengthy and complex statements to fulfill the needs of your application and ultimately your end user. Experienced coders usually add descriptive text to these complex statements for future reference. Such a text is known as comment, and is embedded before or within a SQL statement using two hyphens (--) or is entered within /* and */ character sets.

The first output below displays the use of embedded inline comments entered after two hyphens. The second one, which is used to create multi-line comments to comment out code, is enclosed within /* and */ characters.

Output

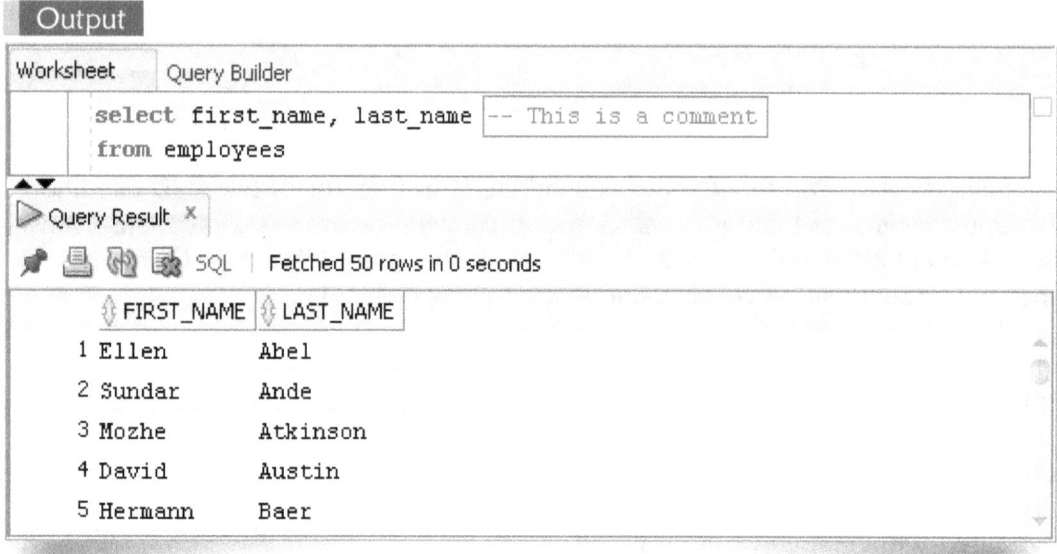

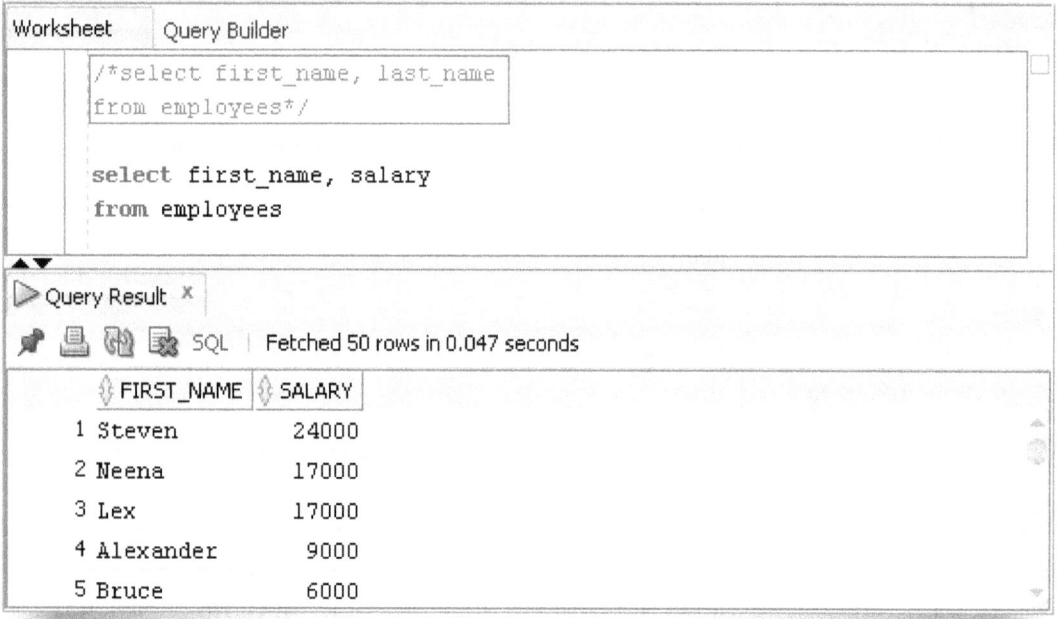

Test Your Skill

1. How would you retrieve all records from the Locations table?

2. Show first name and salary for all employees.

3. Show first name and salary for all employees with salary appearing first.

4. Will the following statement execute successfully? Yes / No

    Select   first_name, job_id, salary Annual _Salary
    From   Employees
    Where first_name = 'Alexander';

5. What about this one? Yes / No

    Select *
    From   Employees
    Where salary * 12 = 72000;

6. Identify the four errors in the following statement:

    Select   first_name, job_id, salary x 12 Annual Salary
    From   Employees
    Where sal = 6000 and hire_date Like %05;

7. Create a query that displays first name, salary, and commission percent for all employees working as sales representatives.

8. Fetch first name, last name, and department number of all employees in department 10 and 20 in alphabetical order of last name. Also, join the two name columns, and set title to Employees.

9. Display a list of all employees containing 'y' in their last names.

10. Display list of employees availing no commission and are enrolled in department number 90.

11. Query the Employees table and fetch names of all employees along with hire dates employed between 1st July 03 and 30th September 03. Display result in ascending order on hire date.

Chapter 3 – Retrieve Data From Database

12. Show names and salaries of all employees who are not making between 3000 and 10000.

13. Write a query that list names and salaries of employees working in department 10, 20, or 30 and earning more than 3000.

14. Display last_name, salary, and commission percent from the Employees table. Calculate annual commission of employees who earn a commission. Use the IN operator in the search condition. Also add an alias to the calculated column.

15. List the name of employees with their hiring dates who were not hired in 2003.

16. Retrieve the DEPARTMENT_ID column for all rows in the Employees table. Suppress duplicate values and sort the output in descending order.

17. Display last name, department number and salary columns from the Employees table for those employees who work either in department number 50 or 90 and also earn more than or equal to 5800.

Chapter 4 – Transform and Summarize Data With Functions

A function can be defined as an operation that is performed with the objective to transform the appearance of data. Like other computer languages, SQL also supports the use of functions to manipulate data. Functions are usually applied to:

- Convert data types of columns
- Data calculation
- Alter display formats
- Provide collective output for groups of rows

Functions are divided into the following two categories:

Single Row functions As the name implies, the functions under this category act only on individual rows, and return a single result for every processed row. You can use these functions in SELECT, WHERE, and ORDER BY clauses. Single row functions are further categorized as follows:

- **Character functions:** These functions accept character data as input and can return both character and number values.
- **Number functions:** Number functions manipulate numeric data. They receive numeric input and return only numeric values.
- **Date functions:** Besides presenting date and time data in some desirable format, these functions are also helpful in comparing date values and computing intervals between dates.
- **Conversion functions:** With the help of these functions you can convert data type of some data to another data type. For example, to concatenate a number value to a character string, you convert the numeric value to character data type.

Aggregate Functions In contrast to the single row functions, the functions under this category operate on groups of rows, and return one result per group. These functions are used to retrieve summarized data for analysis and reporting purposes. In this book, you'll be practicing with the following most common aggregate functions, supported by all platforms.

- Average function – AVG
- Count function – COUNT
- Maximum function – MAX
- Minimum function – MIN
- Sum function – SUM

CONCAT Function

This function is equivalent to the concatenation operator (||) and is used to concatenate first character value to the second character value.

Syntax

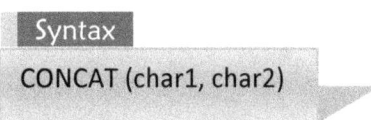

CONCAT (char1, char2)

The following example concatenates first and last names of all employees.

SQL Statement

SELECT   CONCAT(first_name, last_name)
FROM   employees;

Output

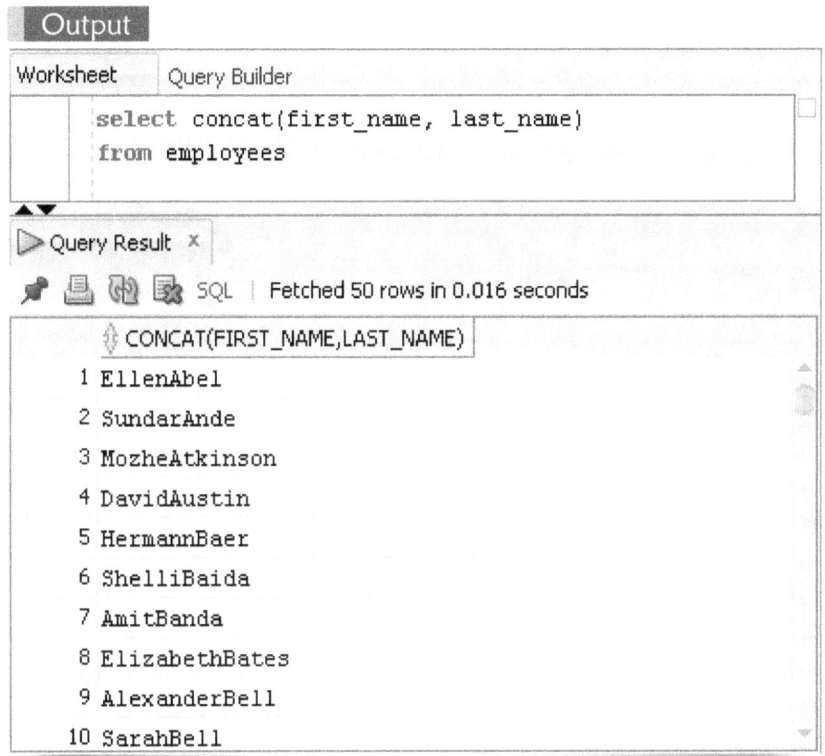

NOTE

In order to put a space between the two names, nest another CONCAT() function into an existing one, like this:

Select CONCAT(CONCAT(first_name, ' '), last_name) Employee From employees;

Consider the following example if you wish to join two column values with some meaningful text in between:

Select CONCAT(CONCAT(last_name, ' is working as '), job_id) "Name and Job" From employees;

Chapter 4 – Transform and Summarize Data With Functions

INITCAP Function

INITCAP returns *character*, with the first letter of each word in uppercase, all other letters in lowercase. The following example converts the first letter of the job id column to uppercase, and the rest to lower case. Note that the values stored in this table column are all upper case.

Syntax

INITCAP (character)

SQL Statement

SELECT	**INITCAP(job_id)**
FROM	employees;

Output

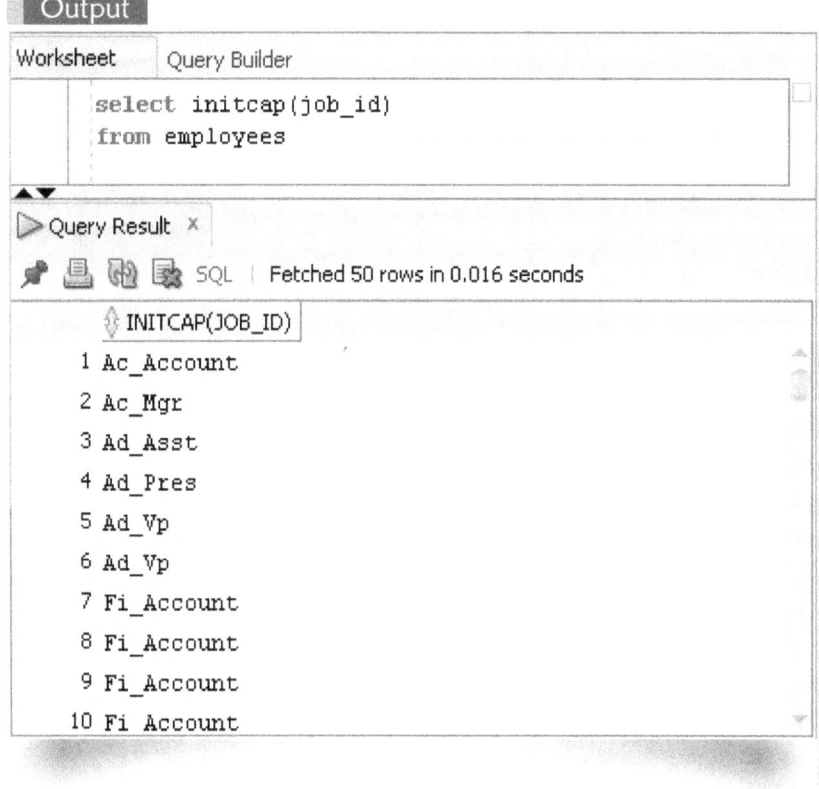

LENGTH Function

The LENGTH function returns the length of character. Note that it is a character function that returns the answer in numbers, as shown in the following example where it is used to count number of character in the first names of employees.

Syntax

LENGTH (character)

NOTE:
In Microsoft SQL Server and Microsoft Access use DATALENGTH() and LEN() functions, respectively.

SQL Statement

SELECT   first_name, **LENGTH(first_name)** Length
FROM   employees;

Chapter 4 – Transform and Summarize Data With Functions

LOWER Function

The LOWER function returns character, with all letters lowercase. The example presented below transforms all data in first name and job id columns to lower case.

Syntax

LOWER (character)

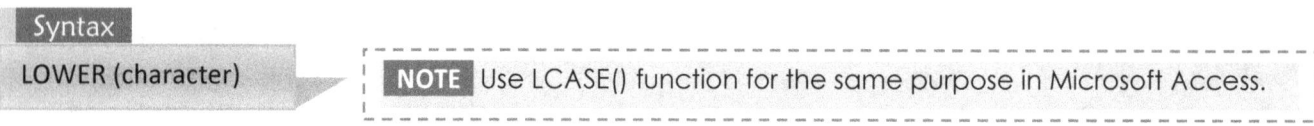

NOTE: Use LCASE() function for the same purpose in Microsoft Access.

SQL Statement

```
SELECT  LOWER(first_name||' '||last_name) Name, LOWER(job_id) Job
FROM    employees;
```

Output

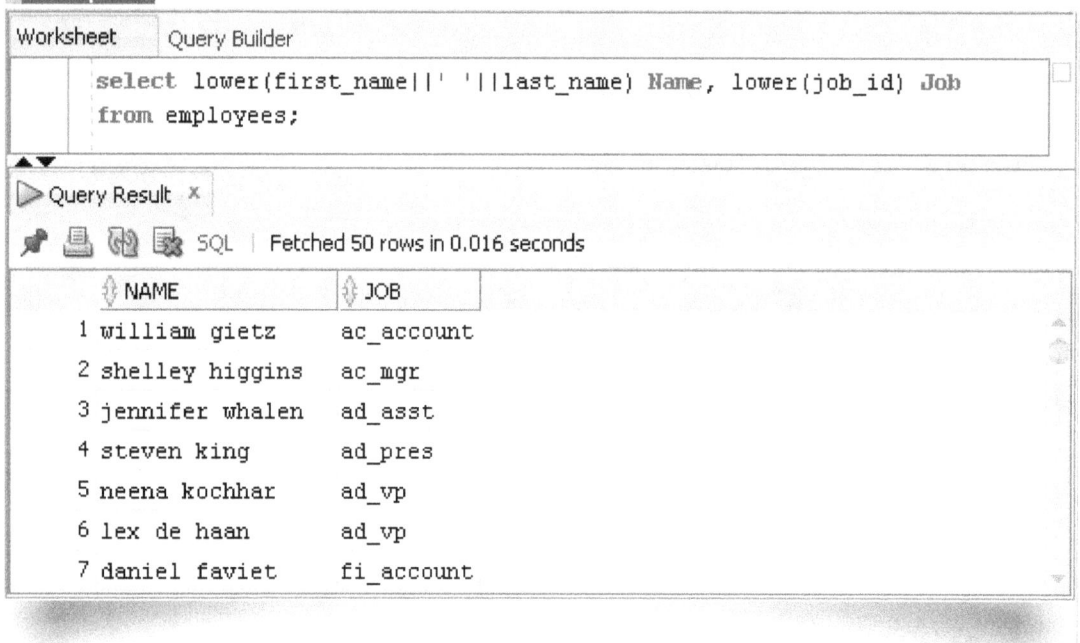

NOTE

As mentioned earlier, single row functions can also be used in the WHERE clause. Let's see an example. Running the first statement below will not yield any result. Change it so that it matches the second statement. Now you'll get some rows. The LOWER() function in the second statement fetched the result, because all the job ids are stored in uppercase in the employees table, and you forced the query (by using the LOWER function) to first convert all the column values to lower case, match each value with the provided lower case string (pu_clerk), and then return the result.

Select first_name, last_name, job_id from employees where job_id='pu_clerk';
Select first_name, last_name, job_id from employees where **lower(job_id)='pu_clerk'**;

NVL Function

When you query a table, the null values stored in a column (e.g commission_pct) are shown as (null). Using the NVL function, you can replace these nulls with some meaningful values. According to the following syntax, if expr1 is null, then NVL returns expr2. If expr1 is not null, then NVL returns expr1. In the following example, you get a list of employees along with their commissions, replacing null values with zero if the employees are not entitled to get commissions.

Syntax

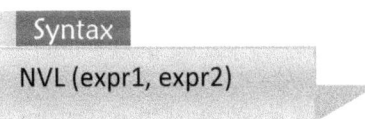

NVL (expr1, expr2)

SQL Statement

```
SELECT   last_name, NVL(commission_pct, 0) commission
FROM     employees
WHERE    last_name LIKE 'B%'
ORDER    BY last_name;
```

Output

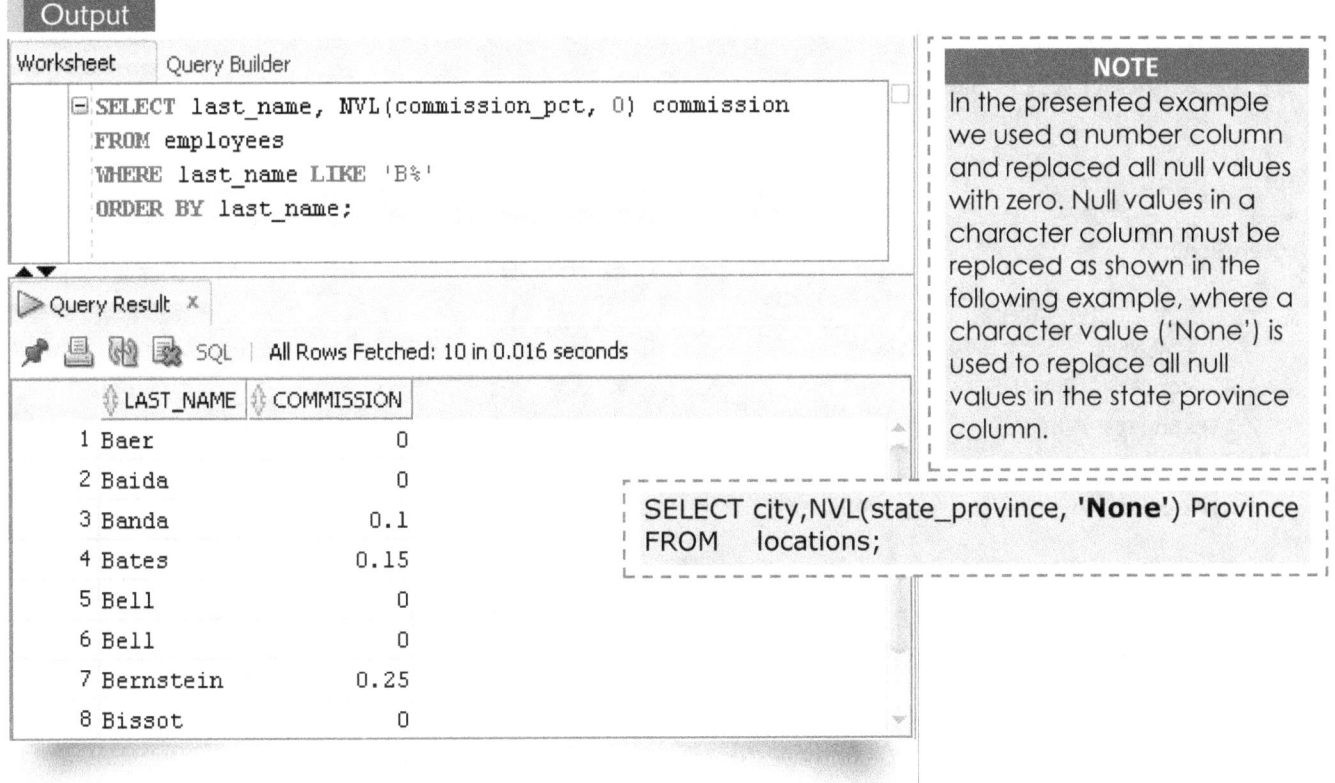

NOTE

In the presented example we used a number column and replaced all null values with zero. Null values in a character column must be replaced as shown in the following example, where a character value ('None') is used to replace all null values in the state province column.

```
SELECT city, NVL(state_province, 'None') Province
FROM    locations;
```

SUBSTR Function

The SUBSTR function returns specified characters from character value, starting from P, L characters long. The following statement fetches records of employees who have 'lex' (three characters) in their names starting from second position.

Syntax

SUBSTR (character, P,L)

SQL Statement

```
SELECT  first_name, last_name, salary
FROM    employees
WHERE   substr(first_name,2,3)='lex';
```

NOTE
In Microsoft Access use MID() function.
In Microsoft SQL Server, MySQL, and MariaDB you have to use SUBSTRING().

Output

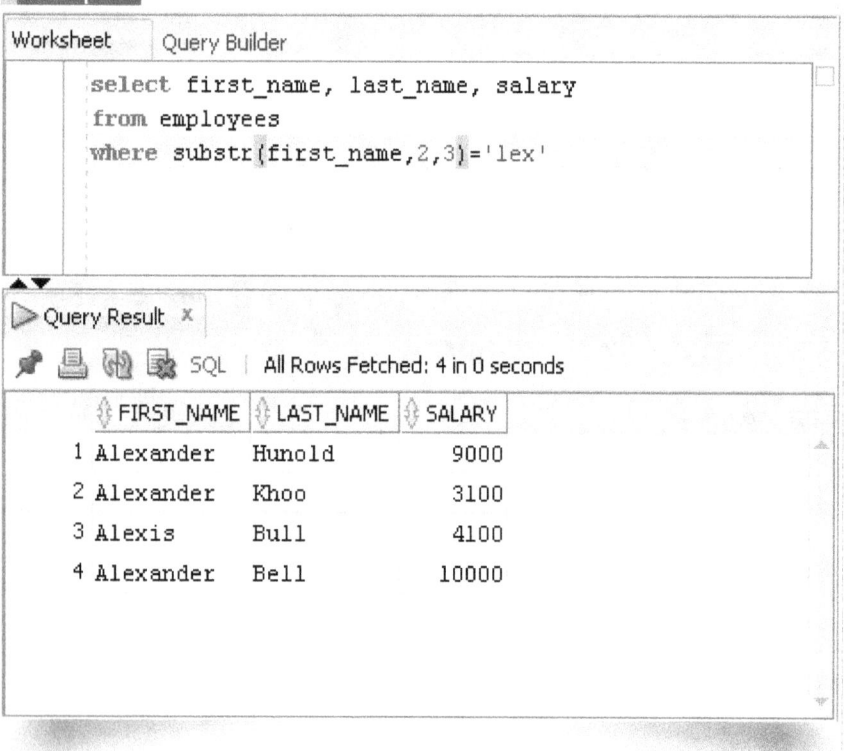

UPPER Function

The UPPER function is contrary to the LOWER function and returns all characters in uppercase letters as shown in the following statement where each employee's first name is displayed in uppercase.

Syntax
UPPER (character)

SQL Statement
```
SELECT  UPPER(first_name)
FROM    employees;
```

NOTE: Microsoft Access uses UCASE() function.

Output

```
select upper(first_name)
from employees;
```

Query Result — Fetched 50 rows in 0.016 seconds

UPPER(FIRST_NAME)
1 ELLEN
2 SUNDAR
3 MOZHE
4 DAVID
5 HERMANN
6 SHELLI
7 AMIT

ROUND Function

ROUND() is a numeric function which rounds the column, expression, or value defined in "n" to "integer" places to the right of the decimal point. If you omit integer, then n is rounded to zero places. If integer is negative, then n is rounded off to the left of the decimal point. n can be any numeric data type or any nonnumeric data type that can be implicitly converted to a numeric data type.

The following statement rounds the value (47.842) to hundredth, zero, and ten decimal places.

Syntax

ROUND (n,integer)

SQL Statement

SELECT   ROUND(47.842,2), ROUND(47.842,0), ROUND(47.842,-1)
FROM   SYS.DUAL;

Output

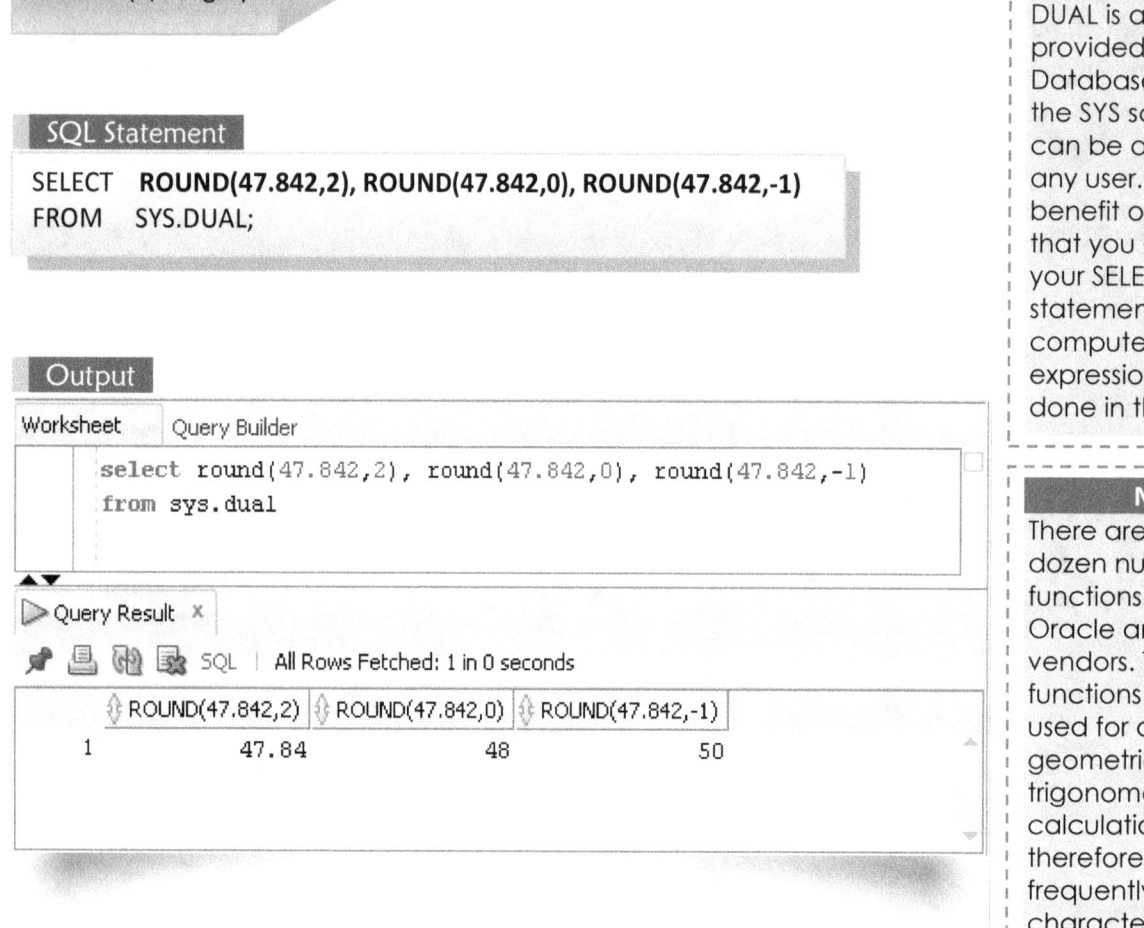

> **NOTE**
> DUAL is a table provided with Oracle Database. It resides in the SYS schema but can be accessed by any user. The major benefit of this table is that you can use it in your SELECT statements to compute constant expressions, as is done in this exercise.

> **NOTE**
> There are over two dozen numeric functions provided by Oracle and other vendors. These functions are primarily used for algebraic, geometric, or trigonometric calculations and, therefore, are not as frequently used as character or date functions.

TRUNC Function

TRUNC() is also a numeric function and works just like the ROUND() function. It returns n1 truncated to n2 decimal places. If n2 is omitted, then n1 is truncated to 0 places. n2 can be negative to truncate (make zero) n2 digits left of the decimal point. Similar to the ROUND() function, it also takes as an argument any numeric data type or any nonnumeric data type that can be implicitly converted to a numeric data type. If you omit n2, then the function returns the same data type as the numeric data type of the argument. If you include n2, then the function returns NUMBER.

Syntax
TRUNC (n1,n2)

SQL Statement
```
SELECT   TRUNC(47.842310,2), TRUNC(47.842310,0), TRUNC(47.842310,-1)
FROM     SYS.DUAL;
```

Output

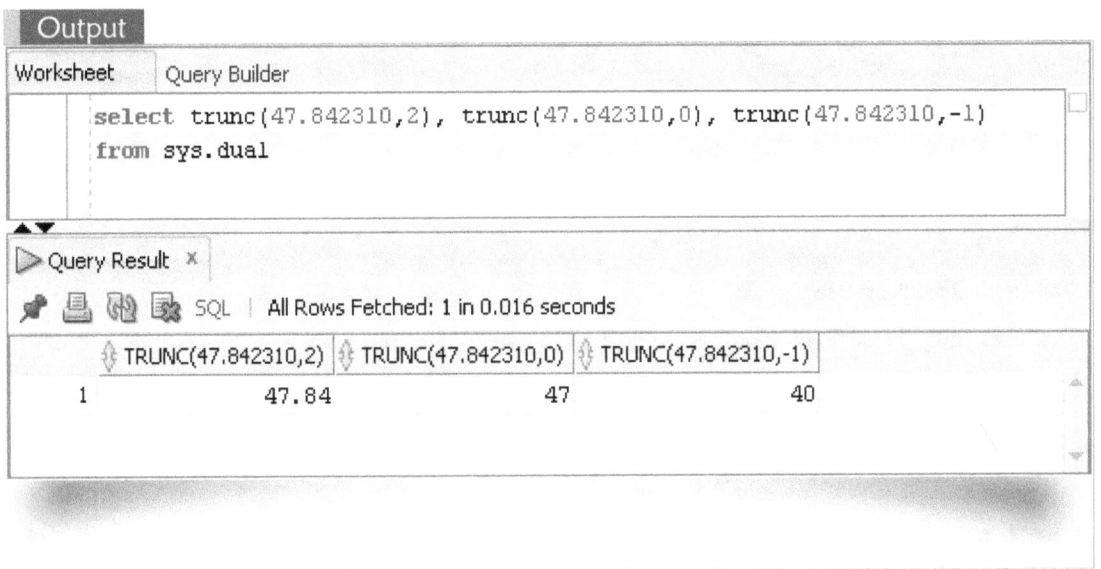

Date Time Functions

Every DBMS allows you to store date and time values in tables using specific date data types and in specific formats. Each implementation follows its own storage format to save the date and time, for example, Oracle's default display and input format for any date is DD-MON-YY. Unfortunately, this default storage varies among different implementations and is, therefore, least portable.

Similar to the character functions, date and time functions are also used to manipulate the representation of data. These function are used not only to present date and time data in some desirable format, but are also helpful in comparing date values, and computing intervals between dates.

To start with, here is an example in Oracle which fetches current date from the system, followed by a list of functions that perform the same task for other platforms.

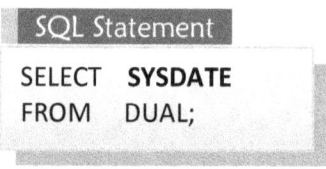

```
SELECT  SYSDATE
FROM    DUAL;
```

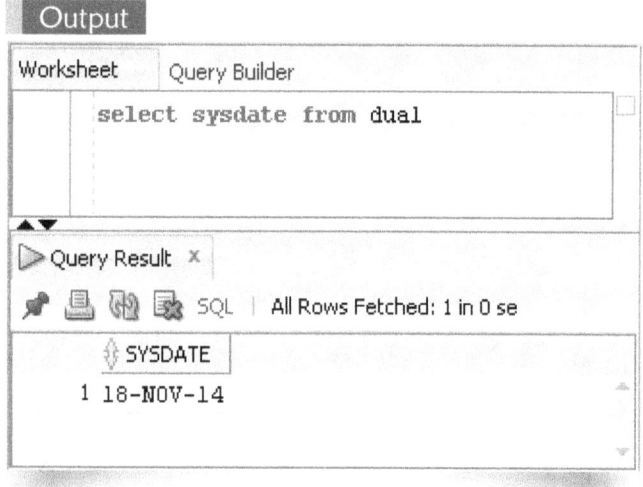

The following table lists respective functions as employed by various DBMSs to get current system date:

DBMS	FUNCTION	SQL STATEMENT	OUTPUT (Format)
MySQL/MariaDB	CURDATE()	SELECT CURDATE();	2014-11-19 *(YYYY-MM-DD)*
PostgreSQL	CURRENT_DATE	SELECT CURRENT_DATE;	2014-11-19 *(YYYY-MM-DD)*
Microsoft Access	NOW()	SELECT Now() FROM Products;	11/19/2014 2:28:17 AM
Microsoft SQL Server	GETDATE()	SELECT GETDATE();	2014-11-19 13:10:02.047
SQLite	DATE()	SELECT DATE('now');	2014-11-19 *(YYYY-MM-DD)*
DB2	CURRENT DATE	SELECT CURRENT DATE FROM sysibm.sysdummy1;	2014-11-19 *(YYYY-MM-DD)*

Date Manipulation Functions

The following examples present date manipulation functions for different implementations, starting with Oracle. The Employees table contains a date column named Hire_Date. All the examples in this section retrieve a list of all employees who were hired in 2003.

The first one below is for Oracle. In this example we used nested functions to first convert the year portion in the hire date column to character – to_char(hire_date,'YYYY'). The character value is then converted to a number with the help of the to_number function, and is matched with the specified year.

SQL Statement

```
SELECT  first_name, hire_date
FROM    employees
WHERE   to_number(to_char(hire_date, 'YYYY')) = 2003;
```

NOTE: TO_NUMBER, TO_CHAR, and TO_DATE are known as conversion functions and will be discussed shortly.

Output

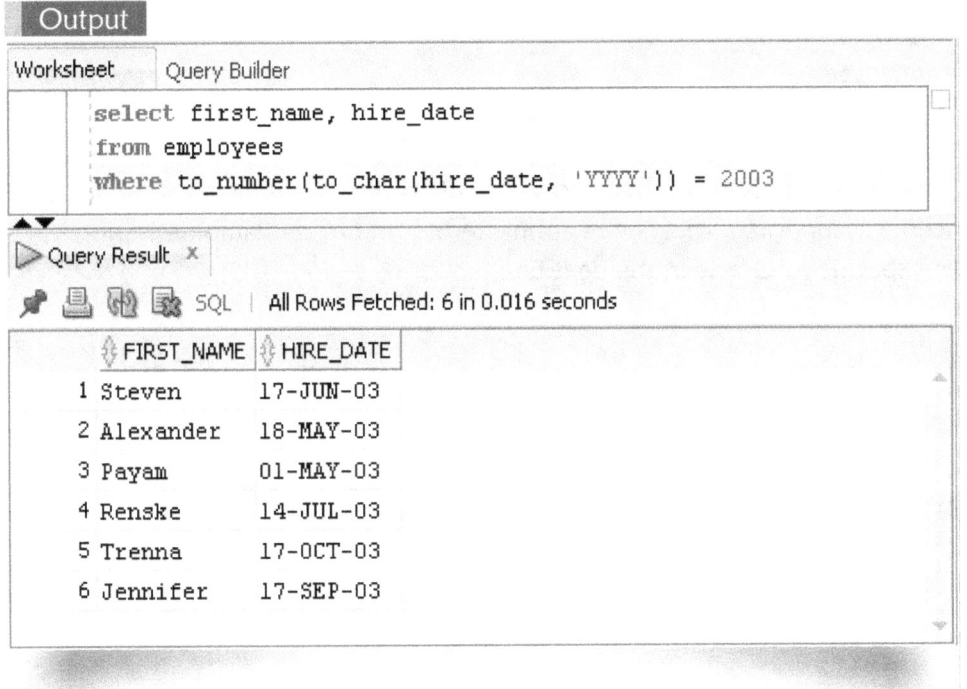

The table that follows describes how you would issue the above statement in other DBMSs to get the same output using platform specific date functions.

Chapter 4 – Transform and Summarize Data With Functions

DBMS	SQL STATEMENT WITH SPECIFIC DATE FUNCTIONS
Alternate in Oracle using the BETWEEN operator	SELECT first_name, hire_date FROM employees WHERE hire_date **BETWEEN** to_date('01-JAN-2003') and to_date('31-DEC-2003');
Microsoft SQL Server	SELECT first_name, hire_date FROM employees WHERE **DATEPART**(yy, hire_date) = 2003;
Microsoft Access	SELECT first_name, hire_date FROM employees WHERE **DATEPART**('yyyy', hire_date) = 2003;
MariaDB and MySQL	SELECT first_name, hire_date FROM employees WHERE **YEAR**(hire_date) = 2003;
SQLite	SELECT first_name, hire_date FROM employees WHERE **strftime**('%Y', hire_date) = 2003;
PostgreSQL	SELECT first_name, hire_date FROM employees WHERE **DATE_PART**('year', hire_date) = 2003;

There is a long list of such functions for each platform. Refer to your DBMS documentation for the list of the date-time manipulation functions it supports. Since we're connected to an Oracle database session, we'll explore some date functions specific to Oracle in the next few sections.

MONTHS_BETWEEN Function

The first date function in Oracle that we'll be experimenting with is the MONTHS_BETWEEN function. As the name implies, this function is useful in determining number of months between two dates. The output of this function can be positive or negative. For the result to be positive, date1 must be later than date2. Conversely, negative result is displayed when date1 is earlier than date2.

Syntax

MONTHS_BETWEEN (date1,date2)

The following example statement evaluates employment tenure in months for employee number 200. The result (134.084...) is based on the difference between the current system date (in my case it is 19-NOV-2014) and the date value stored in the hire date column (i.e. 17-SEP-2003).

SQL Statement

```
SELECT  first_name,hire_date,MONTHS_BETWEEN(sysdate,hire_date) Months_Employed
FROM    employees
WHERE   employee_id=200;
```

Output

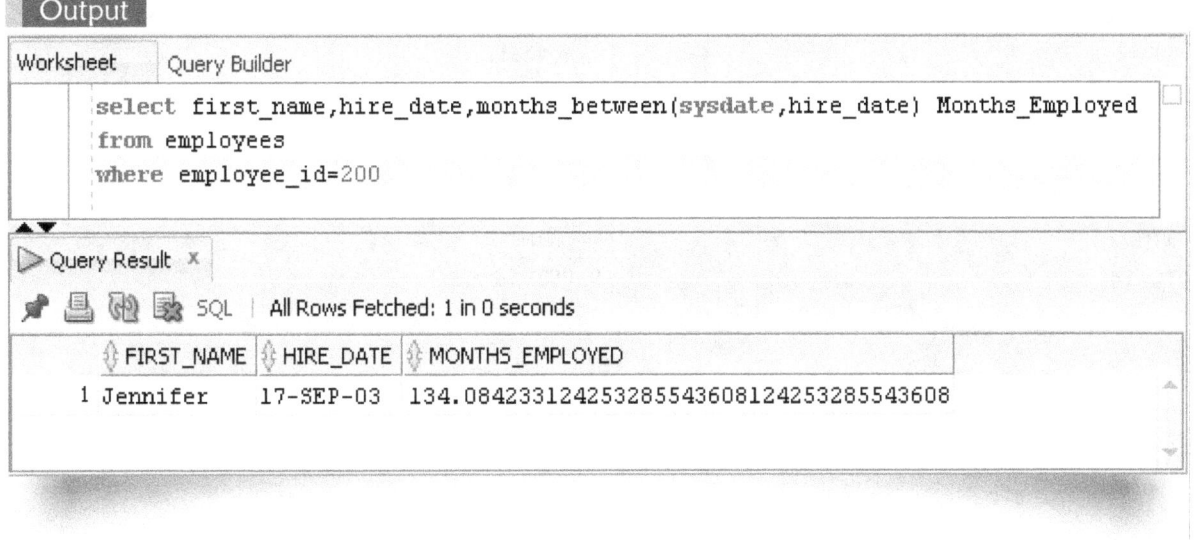

Chapter 4 – Transform and Summarize Data With Functions

ADD_MONTHS Function

Sometimes you need to assess a future date or even a date in the past for some reasons. The ADD_MONTHS function assists you in this kind of calculation. In order to find a future date, add *integer* number of months to the *date*. Similarly, to get previous date, enter a negative value for *integer*, as demonstrated in the following two examples. Note that the system date for both these example is assumed as 19-NOV-2014.

Syntax

ADD_MONTHS (date,integer)

SQL Statement

```
SELECT  ADD_MONTHS(sysdate,1) Month
FROM    dual;
```

```
SELECT  ADD_MONTHS(sysdate,-1) Month
FROM    dual;
```

Output

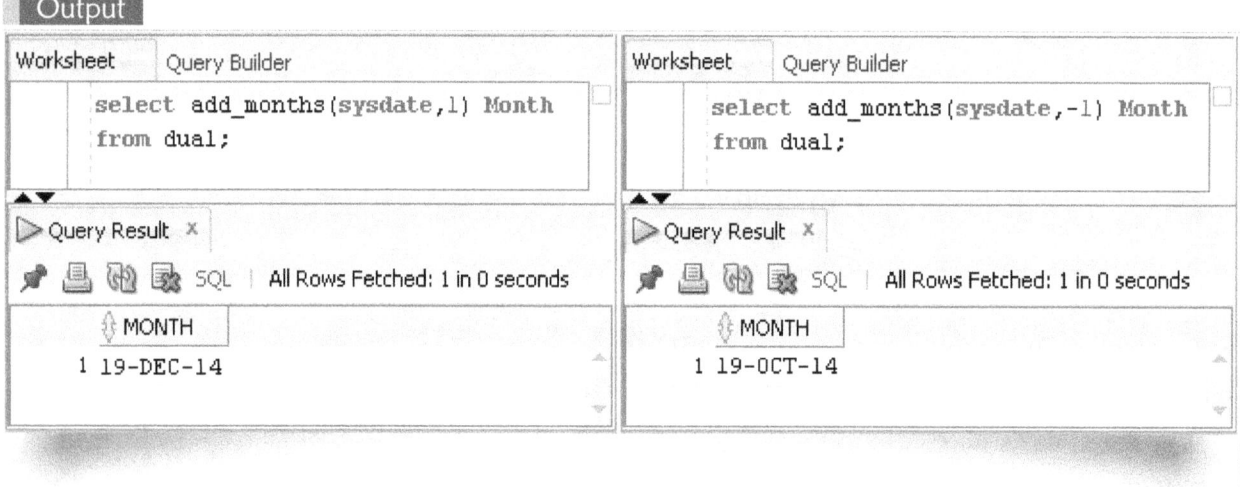

SQL for Everyone

NEXT_DAY Function

The NEXT_DAY function returns the next day of the week specified in *char*. The return type is always date. The argument char must be a day of the week, and can be passed as the full name ('Friday'), an abbreviation ('Fri'), or a number representing a day (6). SYSDATE value in this example too is 19-NOV-2014.

Syntax

NEXT_DAY (date,char)

SQL Statement

```
SELECT   'Next Friday will be on '||NEXT_DAY(sysdate,'Friday') "Next Friday"
FROM     dual;
```

Output

```
select 'Next Friday will be on '||next_day(sysdate,'Friday') "Next Friday"
from dual;
```

Query Result
All Rows Fetched: 1 in 0 seconds

Next Friday
1 Next Friday will be on 21-NOV-14

LAST_DAY Function

The LAST_DAY function returns the date of the last day of the month specified in the **date** argument. The following statement demonstrates two different uses of this function and displays data in three columns. The first one, SYSDATE, returns current system data to supplement the result appearing in the next two columns. The second column shows the last day (30th November) of the current month (based on SYSDATE), while the last one displays the last day of the date specified as character string.

Syntax

LAST_DAY (date)

SQL Statement

```
SELECT   sysdate, LAST_DAY(sysdate), LAST_DAY('16-DEC-14')
FROM     dual;
```

Output

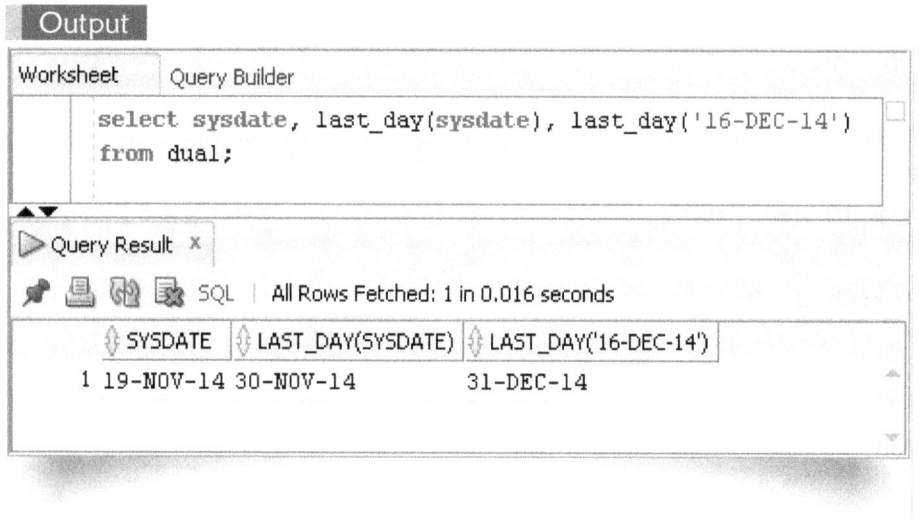

Conversion Functions

Conversion functions allow you to convert a data type into another data type. For example, your table contains some data stored in character format that you want to convert to numeric to perform some mathematical operation. Similarly, you can also covert numeric data to character, but representation of such converted data doesn't support mathematical functions and computations.

You can convert data in the following ways:

1. Date to character
2. Number to character
3. Character to number
4. Character to date

As of this writing, Oracle provides 38 conversion functions to perform various tasks. To keep things simple for the time being, we'll be looking at the following four functions that are most commonly used, and fulfill the four conversion tasks mentioned above.

- TO_CHAR (datetime)
- TO_CHAR (number)
- TO_NUMBER
- TO_DATE

NOTE

In many cases, a database provides its own conversion functions to convert one data type into another. But, there are several occasions when users want to explicitly specify themselves what data type they need to change data into. For such scenarios, SQL includes an ANSI CAST function that converts data types into other data types of your choice. The basic syntax is as follows:

Syntax: CAST (EXPRESSION AS NEW_DATA_TYPE)
Example: SELECT CAST(hire_date AS CHAR(25)) AS "Hired On" FROM employees

---

DATETIME Data Types and Elements

Before we get our feet wet, let's go through some standard data types for date and time. There are three standard SQL data types for date and time storage:

- **DATE:** DATE is formatted as YYYY-MM-DD and ranges from 0001-01-01 to 9999-12-31.
- **TIME:** TIME is formatted as HH:MI:SS.nn... and ranges from 00:00:00... to 23:59:61.999....
- **TIMESTAMP:** TIMESTAMP is formatted as YYYY-MM-DD HH:MI:SS.nn... and ranges from 0001-01-01 00:00:00... to 9999-12-31 23:59:61.999....

The seconds value 61.999 is provided due to the possible insertion or omission of a leap second in a minute.

The following tables list date and time format elements for Oracle. To remind you, in Oracle, the default format to display date values is DD-MON-YY. You have already seen this format in the preceding examples.

Date Elements

ELEMENT	DESCRIPTION	OUTPUT
YYYY	Represents the full year in numbers.	2014
YEAR	Represents the year spelled out.	TWENTY FOURTEEN
MM	Represents the 2 digits value for month.	11
MONTH	Represents the full name of the month.	NOVEMBER
DD	Represents 2 digits day of the month.	20
DY	Represents the 3 letter abbreviation of the day of the week.	THU (for Thursday)
DAY	Represents the full name of the day.	THURSDAY

Time Elements

ELEMENT	DESCRIPTION
AM or PM	Represents meridian indicator.
A.M. or P.M.	Represents meridian indicator with dots.
HH or HH12 or HH24	Represents hour of day or hour (1-12) or hour (0-23).
MI	Represents minutes (0-59).
SS	Represents seconds (0-59).

TO_CHAR (datetime) Function – Oracle

The TO_CHAR(datetime) function is used to covert a date value to a character string. The conversion of dates can take place for any number of reasons. Typical reasons for date conversions are as follows:

- To compare date values of different data types.
- To convert a date value from its default format to one specified by you.

The following query retrieves the system date in 24 hours time format and with full year. Change the query by replacing the elements defined in the previous section and note the outcome. For example, changing the format model to 'fmDD "of" MONTH YYYY' would yield: 20 of November 2014. The fm prefix (which stands for *fill mode*) is added to remove padded blanks.

Syntax
TO_CHAR (datetime,['fmt'])

SQL Statement
```
SELECT  TO_CHAR(SYSDATE, 'DD-MON-YYYY HH24:MI:SS') AS "Current Date"
FROM    dual;
```

Output

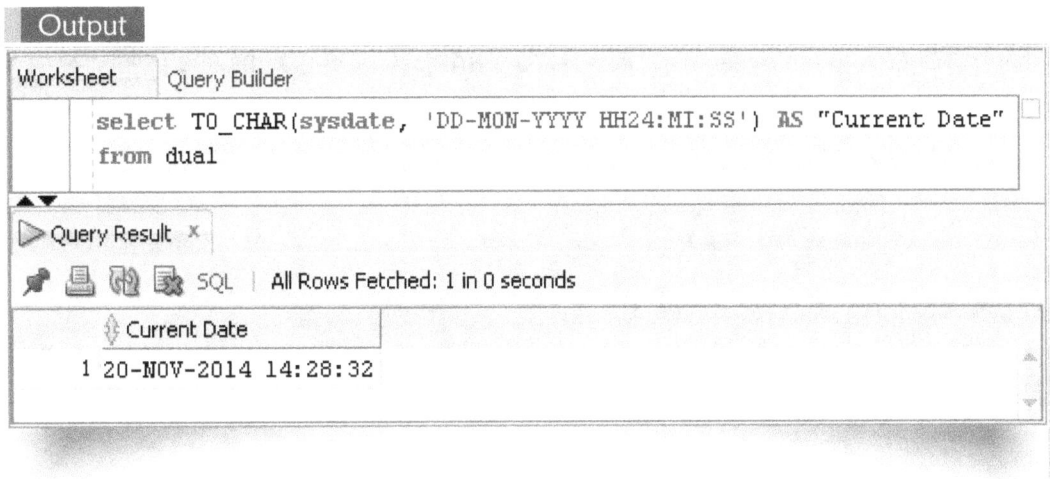

```
Current Date
1  20-NOV-2014 14:28:32
```

NOTE
- The format model (fmt) is case-sensitive (mon will return nov for November).
- Format model must be enclosed in single quotes.
- Use the fill mode (fm) to remove padded blanks or leading zeros.

TO_CHAR (number) Function – Oracle

The TO_CHAR(number) function converts "n" (a number) to a character data type, using the optional number format (fmt). This function is normally utilized when you intend to concatenate number values to a string, as demonstrated in the example below where a complete sentence is generated by concatenating two numeric values (employee id and salary) to character strings. Use the elements listed in the following table to set the output format.

Number Elements

ELEMENTS	DESCRIPTION	EXAMPLE	RESULT
9	Represents numeric position and determines display width.	999999	1234
0	Used to display leading zeros.	099999	001234
$	Displays values with a leading dollar sign.	$999999	$1234
.	Places a decimal point in the specified position.	999999.99	1234.00
,	Positions commas in defined positions.	999,999	1,234
MI	Returns negative value with a trailing minus sign (-).	999999MI	1234-
PR	Returns negative value in <angle brackets>.	999999PR	<1234>

Syntax

TO_CHAR (n,['fmt'])

SQL Statement

SELECT 'Employee number '||**TO_CHAR(employee_id)**||' gets '||**TO_CHAR(salary,'fm$9,999,999')** "Salaries"
FROM employees;

Output

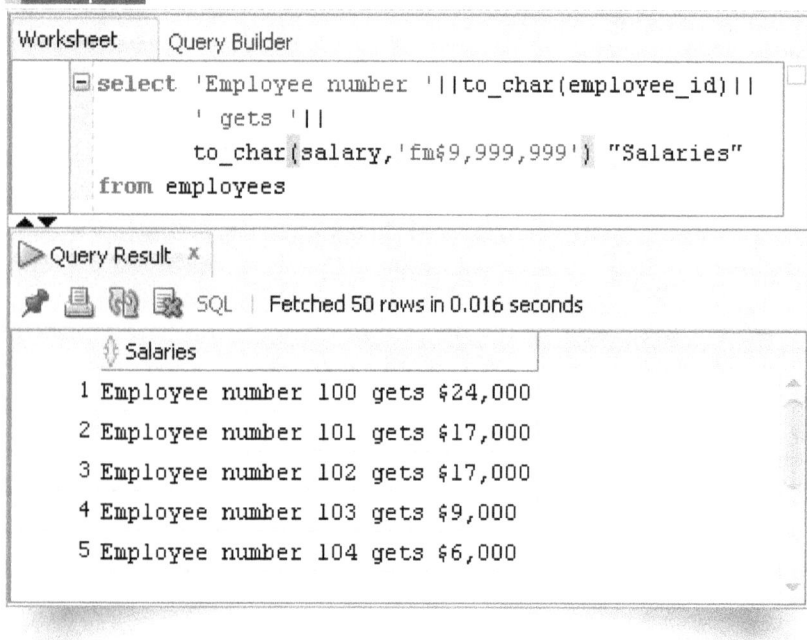

TO_NUMBER Function – Oracle

TO_NUMBER converts a character expression (*expr*) to a value of NUMBER data type. For a character string to be converted to a number, the expr must typically be 0 through 9. For example, the string HELLO cannot be converted to a number, whereas postal/zip codes stored as character string in a table can be converted to numbers using this function. You can also use (+),(-), and (.) symbols to represent positive, negative, and decimal values. The following statement calculates an incremented salary for employee number 200 by converting and then adding a character value ('600.00') to actual salary. In order to reduce the salary, enter a negative number like this: -600.00.

Syntax

TO_NUMBER (expr,['fmt'])

SQL Statement

SELECT salary, salary+**TO_NUMBER('600.00')** "INCREMENTED SALARY"
FROM employees
WHERE employee_id=200;

Output

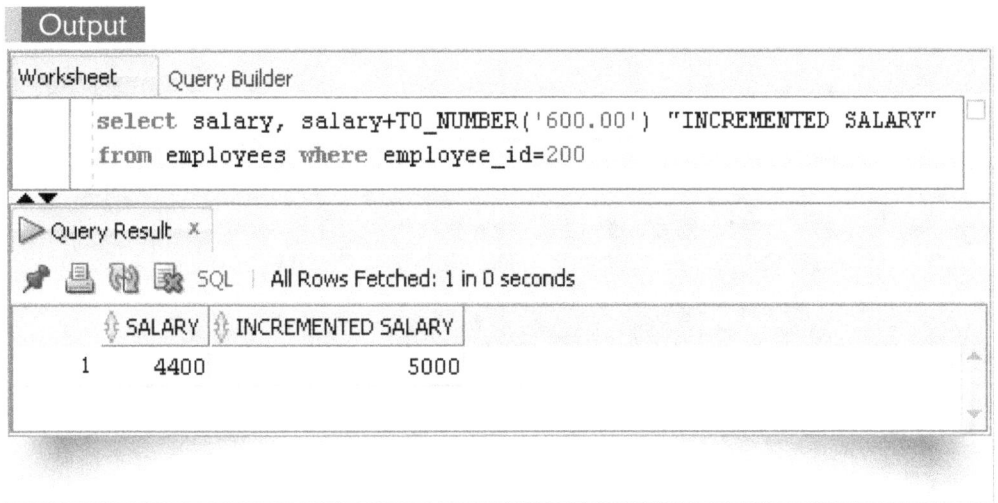

Chapter 4 – Transform and Summarize Data With Functions

TO_DATE Function – Oracle

TO_DATE converts character data type (*char*) to a value of DATE data type. The fmt is a datetime model format specifying the format of char. It is good practice always to specify a format mask (fmt) with TO_DATE, as shown in the example that follows. The statement fetches record of an employee who was hired on March 3, 2005. The TO_DATE function converts the char value ('March 3, 2005') into date data type, formats it as 'Month DD, YYYY', and then compares it to the hire date column value in the employees table. The output date is presented in the default format. If you wish to also see the output in the same format, change the hire_date column in the SELECT clause like this:
TO_CHAR(hire_date,'fmMonth DD, YYYY') "HIRE DATE".

Syntax

TO_DATE (char,['fmt'])

SQL Statement

SELECT   first_name, salary, hire_date
FROM   employees
WHERE   hire_date=**TO_DATE('March 3, 2005','Month DD, YYYY')**;

Output

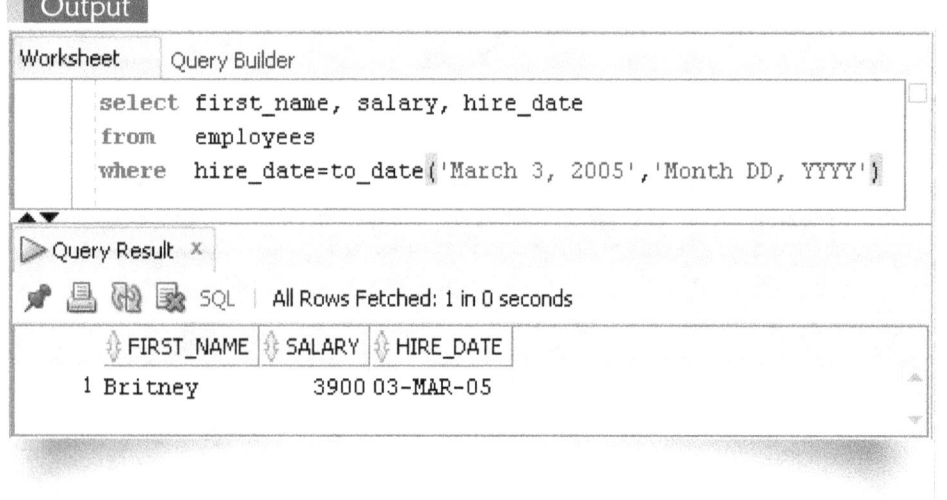

SQL for Everyone

Calculating Dates

Since dates are stored as numbers in database table, you can perform calculations on date values using common arithmetic operators like (+), (-), and (/), as mentioned in the following table. The date value for SYSDATE in the Example column is assumed to be 21-NOV-2014 (12PM).

Operation	Description	Result	Example
Date + Number	Add number of days to a date.	Date	SYSDATE+5 returns 26-NOV-14
Date – Number	Subtract number of days from a date.	Date	SYSDATE-5 returns 16-NOV-14
Date – Date	Subtract one date from another to find number of days between those dates.	Number of days	SYSDATE-to_date('01-NOV-14') returns 20.50
Date + Number/24	Add number of hours to a date.	Date	SYSDATE+24/24 returns 22-NOV-14

The following example returns number of employment weeks for each employee by using the division arithmetic operator.

SQL Statement

```
SELECT  first_name, (sysdate-hire_date)/4 "WEEKS"
FROM    employees;
```

Output

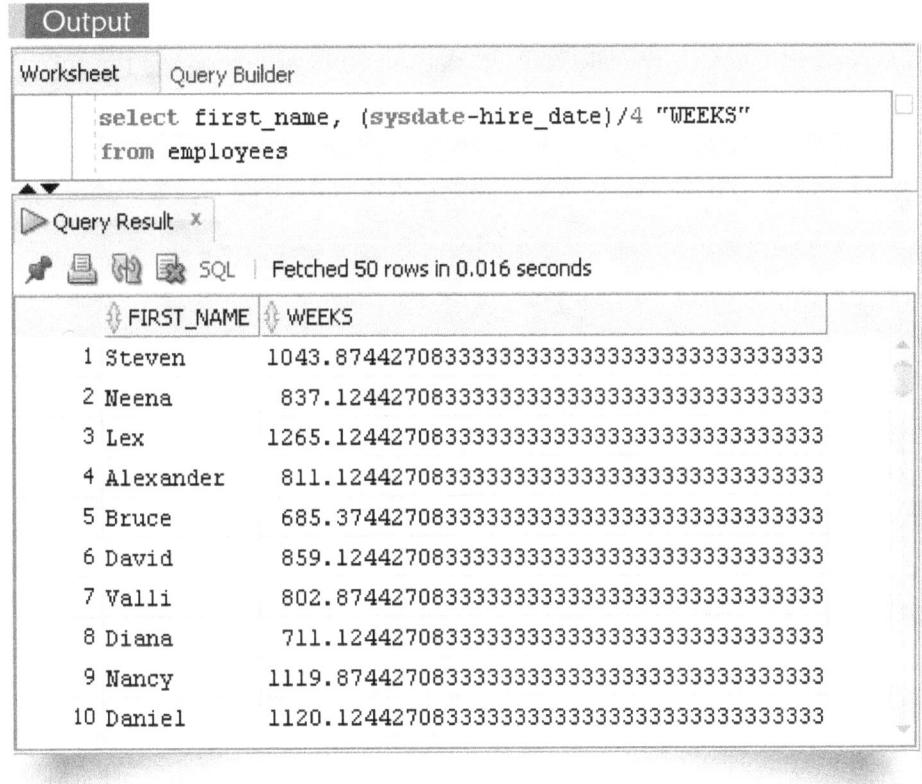

Aggregate Functions

The focus of this section is on how data can be grouped and aggregated to allow you to interact with it at some higher level of granularity than what is stored in the database, using aggregate functions. Aggregate functions return a single result row based on groups of rows, rather than on single rows. You use these functions in your SQL queries to retrieve data for analysis and reporting purposes. For example, you can use these functions to:

- Evaluate total number of records in a table, or number of rows that meet some specific criteria.
- Retrieve summary information such as total, average, highest, or lowest value from a table column.

You'll use the following aggregate functions in the upcoming sections to achieve the objectives mentioned above. Note that unlike single row functions, these aggregate functions are supported by all SQL implementations.

FUNCTION	SYNTAX
AVG	AVG([DISTINCT|ALL]|expr)
COUNT	COUNT([DISTINCT|ALL]|expr)
MAX	MAX([DISTINCT|ALL]|expr)
MIN	MIN([DISTINCT|ALL]|expr)
SUM	SUM([DISTINCT|ALL]|expr)

Aggregate functions are usually added to the SELECT list, but can also appear in ORDER BY and HAVING clauses. They are commonly used in conjunction with the GROUP BY clause in a query to divide the rows of a queried table into groups.

AVG() Function

The AVG() function is used to obtain the average value of data in a specific column. The function calculates the average value by dividing the sum of values in the specified column by the number of rows in the table. This function takes as an argument any numeric data type or any nonnumeric data type that can be implicitly converted to a numeric data type. The first statement below uses the AVG() function in its simplest form to return the average salaries of all employees as a single value.

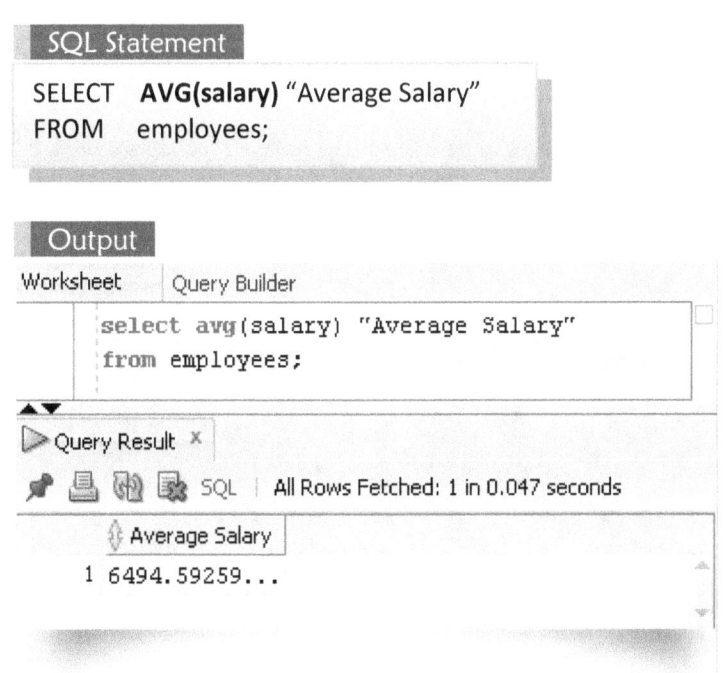

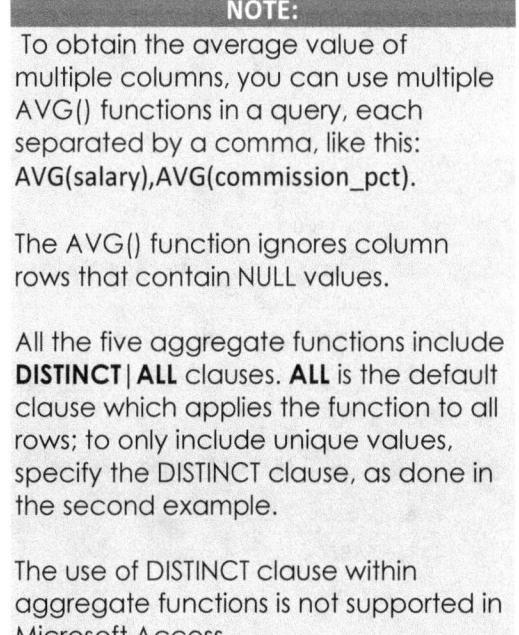

> **NOTE:**
> To obtain the average value of multiple columns, you can use multiple AVG() functions in a query, each separated by a comma, like this: AVG(salary),AVG(commission_pct).
>
> The AVG() function ignores column rows that contain NULL values.
>
> All the five aggregate functions include **DISTINCT|ALL** clauses. **ALL** is the default clause which applies the function to all rows; to only include unique values, specify the DISTINCT clause, as done in the second example.
>
> The use of DISTINCT clause within aggregate functions is not supported in Microsoft Access.

In the following example, a higher average salary is returned due to the use of DISTINCT clause. There are multiple salaries with the same values in the Employees table, therefore, excluding these duplicates resulted in a higher average.

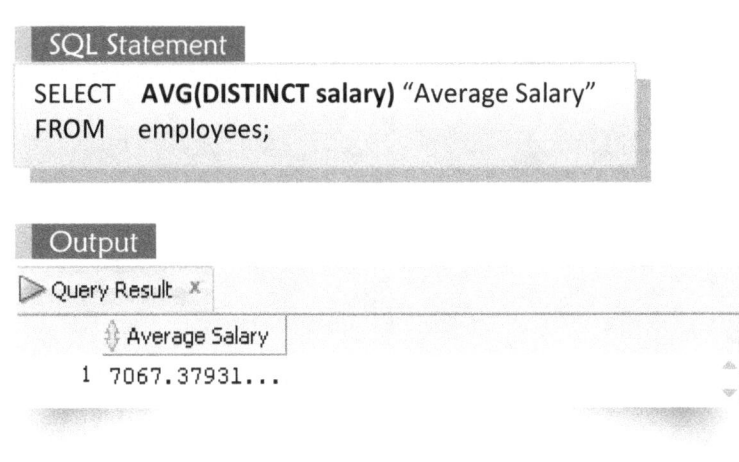

AVG() Function (continued)

Using the AVG() function you can also assess the average value of some specific criteria. For example, the following query determines the average salary of employees in department number 50. This filtration is based on the WHERE clause which filters only salaries for employees working in the specified department.

SQL Statement

```
SELECT  AVG(salary) "Average Salary"
FROM    employees
WHERE   department_id=50;
```

Output

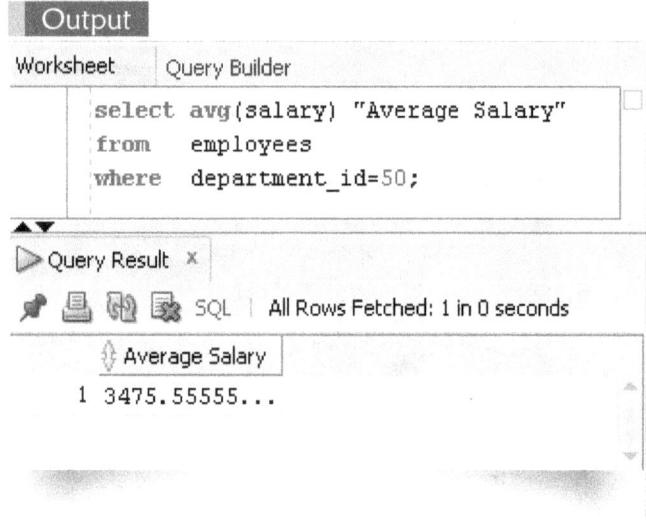

COUNT() Function

As the name implies, the COUNT() function counts total rows in a table or it returns number of rows for the criterion specified in *expr*. You can use this function in the following two formats:

COUNT(*): It counts the number of rows in a table, including duplicate rows and rows containing null values.

COUNT(expr): It returns the count of non-null rows in the column specified in expr.

The first example here counts all rows, irrespective of values, and returns the total number of records in the Employees table:

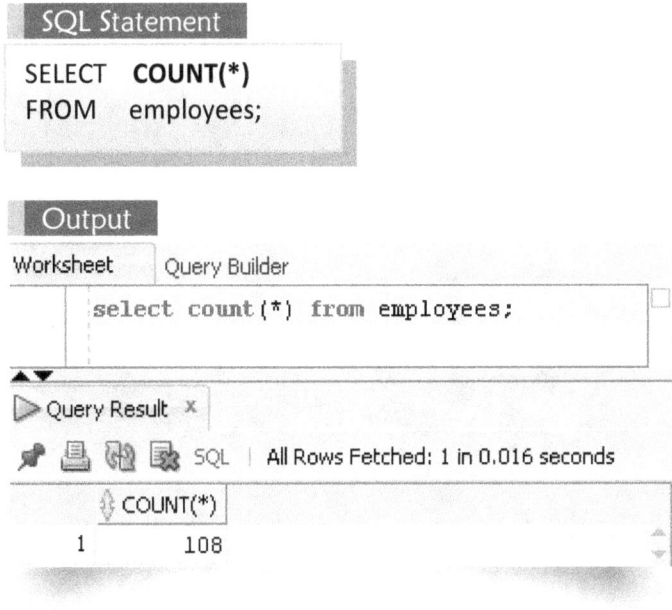

This one counts the number of employees who are entitled to get commission. To narrows the result further, you can add the WHERE clause to these statements, like this: WHERE department_id=80.

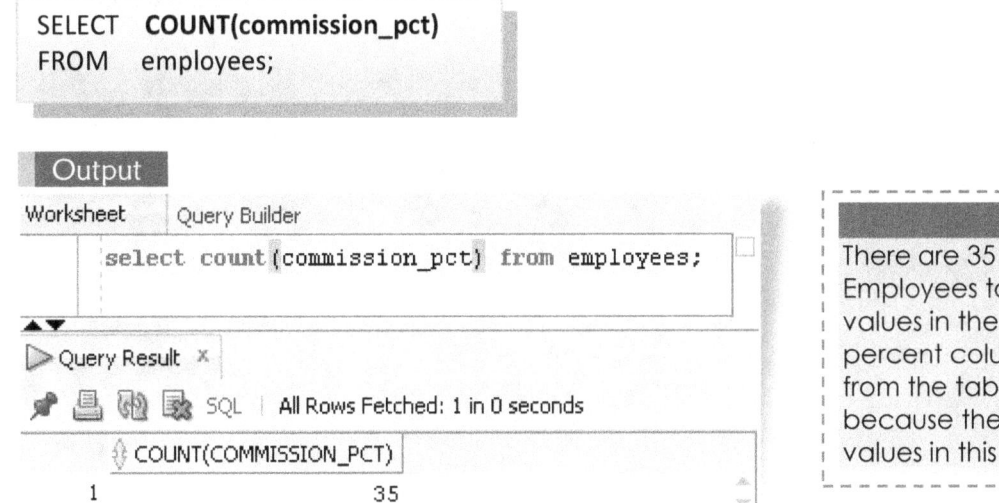

NOTE: There are 35 such records in the Employees table that carry values in the commission percent column. Other records from the table are eliminated, because they all have null values in this column.

MIN() and MAX() Functions

These two functions are used to get highest and lowest values from a column. A general perception is that these two functions are used to only retrieve high and low numeric values, which is not correct. In fact, you can apply them to date data and even to character values, as demonstrated in the following examples.

SQL statement to obtain high and low NUMERIC data

```
SELECT  MIN(salary) "Minimum", MAX(salary) "Maximum"
FROM    employees;
```

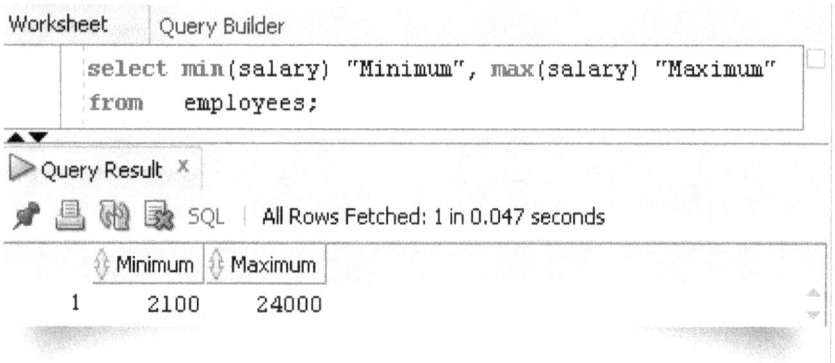

SQL statement to obtain high and low DATE data

```
SELECT  MIN(hire_date) "Minimum", MAX(hire_date) "Maximum"
FROM    employees;
```

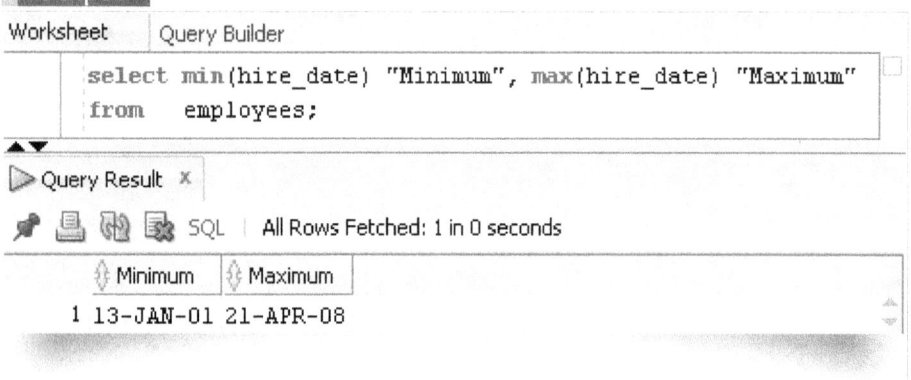

The following example shows how you can apply high and low values to a character column. In this statement we applied the two functions on the first name column to fetch alphabetized high and low values.

SQL statement to obtain high and low CHARACTER data

SELECT   MIN(first_name) "Minimum", MAX(first_name) "Maximum"
FROM   employees;

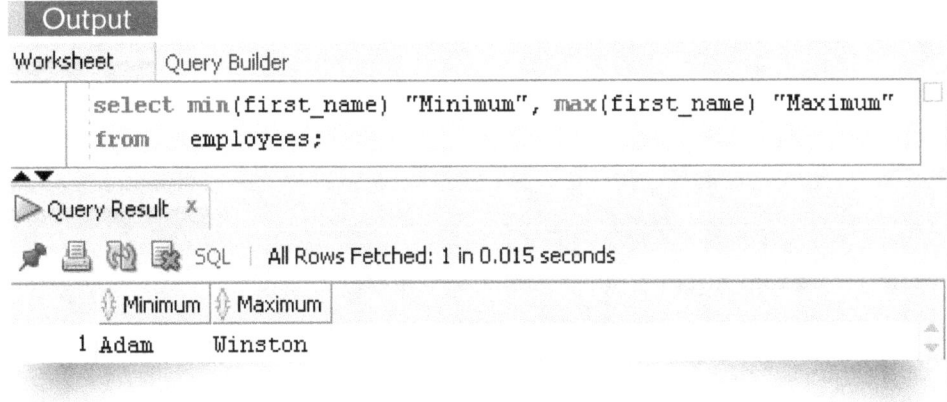

Aggregate functions can also be nested into each other. For example, the following statement calculates the average of the maximum salaries of all the departments. The GROUP BY function will be discussed in a while.

SQL Statement

SELECT   AVG(MAX(salary))
FROM   employees
GROUP BY department_id ;

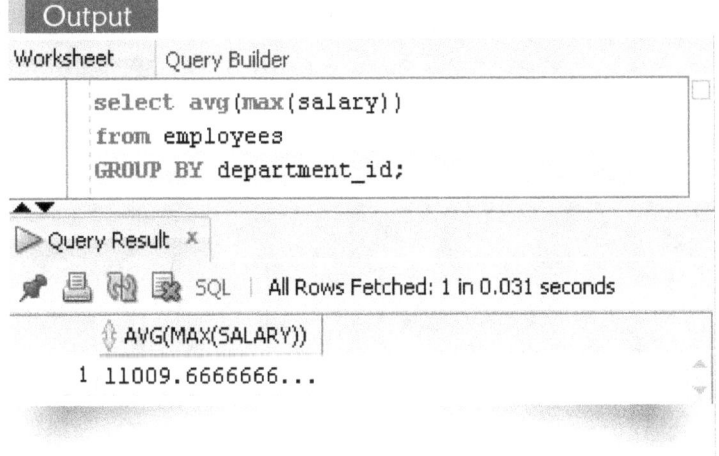

SUM() Function

The SUM function returns the total of values of *expr*. The first function in the following example statement - SUM(salary) – is applied to a table column (salary) to calculate the total amount of salaries being paid in department number 80, while the second function - SUM(salary * commission_pct) – is an expression that retrieves the total amount of commission being paid in this department by multiplying each salary with each value in the commission percent column.

SQL Statement

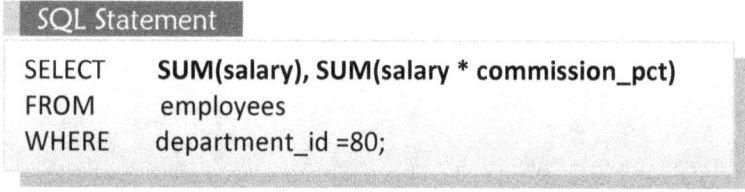

```
SELECT    SUM(salary), SUM(salary * commission_pct)
FROM      employees
WHERE     department_id =80;
```

Output

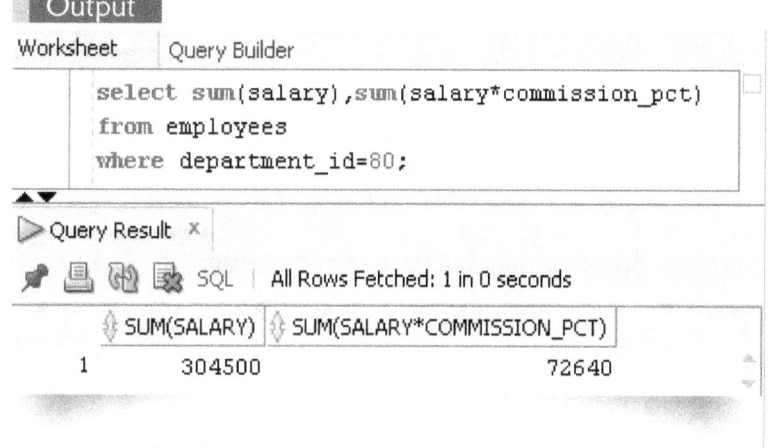

SQL for Everyone

Aggregate Functions Used Together

So far, you have used aggregate functions individually (except for one used in the nested example). A specific situation may demand the use of all these functions in a single statement. Have a look at it in the following example which presents a complete summarized picture of the Employees table by congregating all the five functions in a single statement with respective return values.

SQL Statement

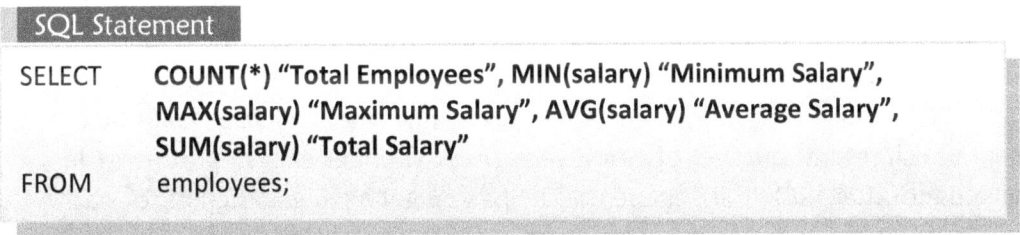

```
SELECT    COUNT(*) "Total Employees", MIN(salary) "Minimum Salary",
          MAX(salary) "Maximum Salary", AVG(salary) "Average Salary",
          SUM(salary) "Total Salary"
FROM      employees;
```

Output

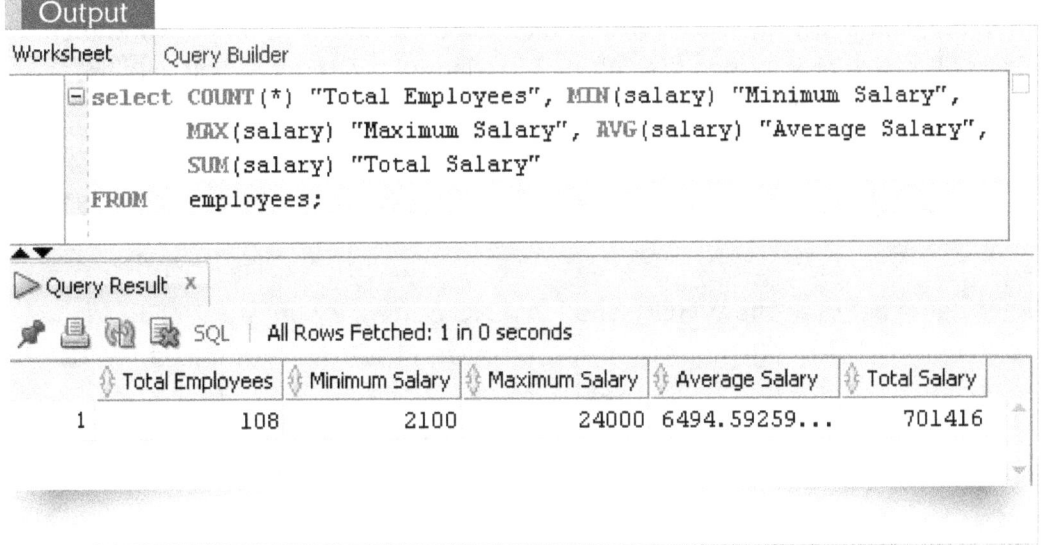

The GROUP BY Clause

The SELECT syntax contains two more clauses: GROUP BY and HAVING. In the next few sections, you'll go through the use of these two important clauses, starting with the GROUP BY clause. The GROUP BY clause is used in a SELECT statement to divide the rows in a table into smaller groups. Aggregate functions are commonly used with this clause to produce summarized subsets of data. DBMSs apply the aggregate functions to each group of rows and return a single result row for each group. If this clause is omitted, then the aggregate functions are applied to all rows in the queried table - as you saw in the previous sections. For example, in the COUNT() function example you executed the statement (*SELECT COUNT(*) FROM EMPLOYEES;*) to get total number of employees from the table. But what will you do if you are asked to prepare a statement which returns number of employees working under each department? In situations like this, you make use of the GROUP BY clause that helps you get aggregate figures for each group. Let's go through an example to handle the problem situation.

In the example presented on the next page, the DBMS groups the data by department number and then calculates the aggregate figures for each group using the GROUP BY clause. As a result, employees are counted for each department rather than for the entire table. The output shows 45 employees in department number 50 and 1 employee in department number 10.

Guidelines for the GROUP BY clause

- Place the GROUP BY clause between the WHERE and HAVING clauses. By using a WHERE clause, you pre-exclude rows before dividing them into groups, whereas, HAVING filters data after the groups are formed.

- The current example uses just one column in the GROUP BY clause. However, you can create nested groups by adding as many columns as you need.

- Leaving the column used in the aggregate function, you must include all the columns or expressions (specified in the SELECT list) in the GROUP BY clause.

- If the grouping column contains a row with a NULL value, a separate NULL group will be created for such record. See record number 12 in the output screenshot on the next page. This null group is created because the department number is not specified in the table.

SQL for Everyone

SQL Statement

```
SELECT    department_id "Department", Count(*) "Number of Employees"
FROM      employees
GROUP BY  department_id
ORDER BY  department_id;
```

Output

```
SELECT    department_id "Department", COUNT(*) "Number of Employees"
FROM      employees
GROUP BY  department_id
ORDER BY  department_id;
```

Query Result — All Rows Fetched: 12 in 0 seconds

#	Department	Number of Employees
1	10	1
2	20	2
3	30	6
4	40	1
5	50	45
6	60	6
7	70	1
8	80	34
9	90	3
10	100	6
11	110	2
12	(null)	1

Using WHERE and GROUP BY Together

As stated above, you can use a WHERE clause in a SELECT statement along with the GROUP BY clause to pre-exclude rows before dividing them into groups. For this, the WHERE clause must be placed before the GROUP BY clause. Here is an example which uses both these clauses together to display a list of job categories and total monthly salaries for each category, excluding the sales force: SA_MAN and SA_REP.

As you can see, the WHERE clause is used before GROUP BY and carries a condition to exclude irrelevant rows. The condition excludes the two categories of employees (Sales Managers and Sales Representatives), mentioned above. Also note the ORDER BY clause which uses the expression (specified in the SELECT list) to sort the output.

SQL Statement

```
SELECT    job_id "Job Category", sum(salary) "Salary"
FROM      employees
WHERE     job_id NOT LIKE 'SA%'
GROUP BY  job_id
ORDER BY  sum(salary);
```

Output

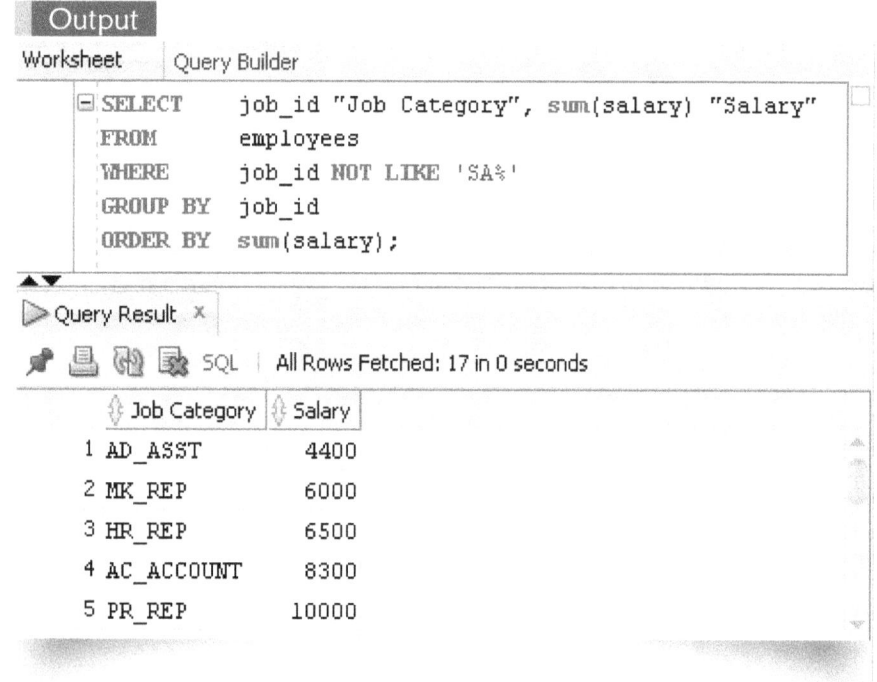

WHERE vs. HAVING

WHERE should be used for standard filtering, and HAVING (discussed next) must be used with GROUP BY to restrict groups. You cannot use the WHERE clause to restrict groups. The following two examples further elaborates these principles:

Incorrect:
select department_id,
        AVG(salary)
from   employees
where   AVG(salary)>5000
group by department_id;

Correct:
select department_id,
        AVG(salary)
from   employees
group by department_id
having AVG(salary)>5000;

The HAVING Clause

As stated above, the HAVING clause restricts the groups of returned rows to those matching the specified condition. If you omit this clause, then the DBMS returns summarized result for all groups, as you saw in the example presented on Page 79. The DBMS performs the following steps when it sees this clause in a SELECT statement:

- Exclude rows not satisfying the WHERE clause.
- Transforms rows into groups.
- Applies the group function.
- Displays the groups for which the condition specified in the HAVING clause is true.

You already went through an example of this clause presented on the previous page; let's have some more on this. The following example was also demonstrated on the previous page, and is repeated here by adding the HAVING clause to further restrict the result on the basis of aggregate information. Compare the result of this statement with the previous one. The HAVING clause condition eliminated the first three groups that appeared in the previous result.

SQL Statement

```
SELECT     job_id "Job Category", sum(salary) "Salary"
FROM       employees
WHERE      job_id NOT LIKE 'SA%'
GROUP BY   job_id
HAVING     sum(salary) >= 8300
ORDER BY   sum(salary);
```

Output

All Rows Fetched: 14 in 0.016 seconds

	Job Category	Salary
1	AC_ACCOUNT	8300
2	PR_REP	10000
3	PU_MAN	11000
4	AC_MGR	12008
5	FI_MGR	12008
6	MK_MAN	13000
7	PU_CLERK	13900

One more thing that needs to be clarified with respect to the GROUP BY and HAVING clauses is that, the GROUP BY clause can be used without using any aggregation function in the SELECT list. In the following example, both these clauses exist without using any aggregation function in the SELECT list. Because the SUM aggregate function is referenced in the HAVING clause, the GROUP BY clause is also specified.

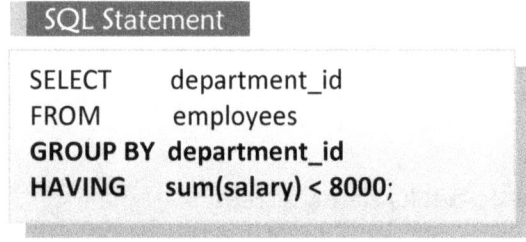

```
SELECT     department_id
FROM       employees
GROUP BY   department_id
HAVING     sum(salary) < 8000;
```

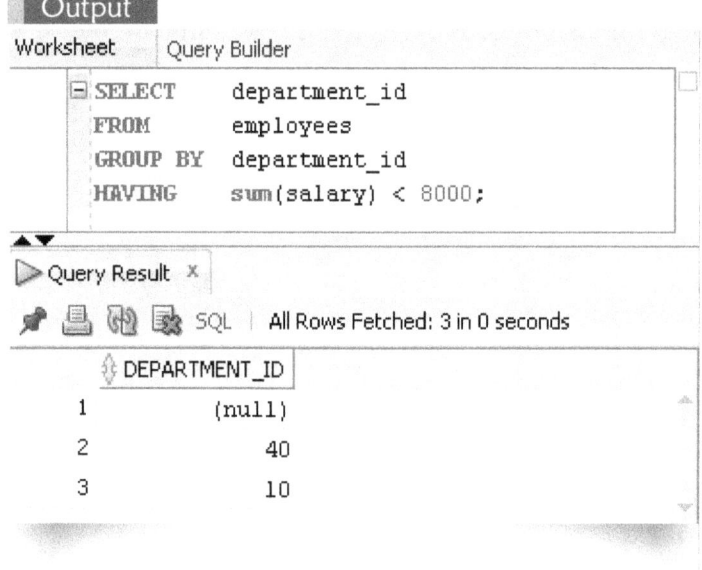

Test Your Skill

1. Create a query that calculates 10% incremented salary for each employee. Display the new values under the name "INCREMENTED_SALARY" and as whole numbers.

   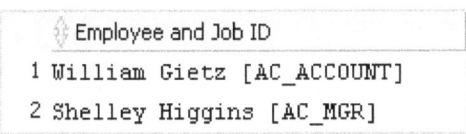

2. Create a query that produces the following output for all employees. Use the CONCAT function to join names.

   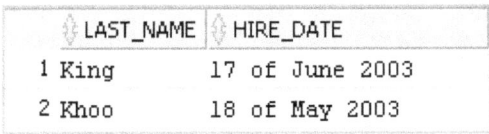

3. Create a query to display last name of employees with hire date as follows. Restrict the output to those who were hired in 2003.

   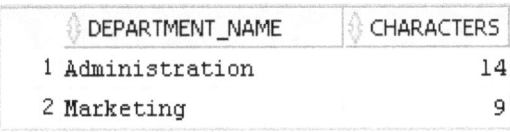

4. Count number of characters in each department's name as shown below:

   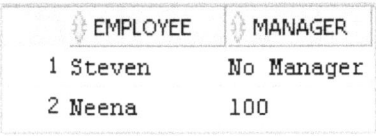

5. Provide a list of employees as illustrated below. The output displays the first name of each employee with his/her manager number. If the manager number is null, display a text "No Manager" instead.

   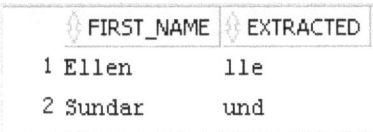

6. Pick three letters from the first name of each employee starting from the second position, like this:

FIRST_NAME	EXTRACTED
1 Ellen	lle
2 Sundar	und

7. Display hire dates of Jennifer in yyyy.dd.mon format.

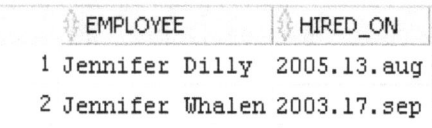

8. Produce the following list which displays employees whose employment tenure is greater than 100 months.

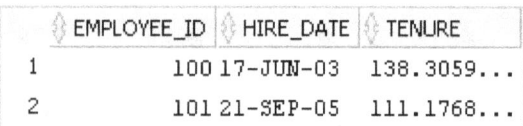

9. Create a statement to display the number of employees for each job category within each department.

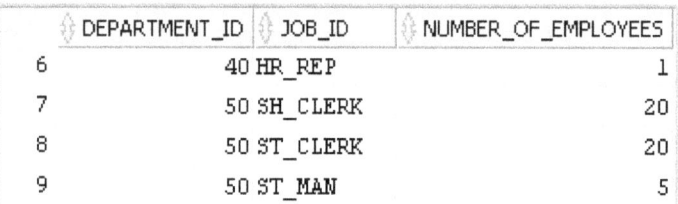

10. Display the minimum salary for each job id having a minimum salary more than 15000.

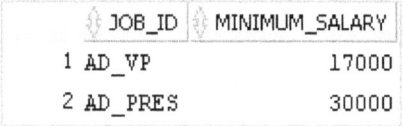

Subqueries

5

Chapter 5 – Subqueries

What are Subqueries?

A query is an operation that retrieves data from one or more tables or views. In the current context, a top-level SELECT statement is called main query, and a query nested within a clause of the main query is called a subquery, as illustrated in the following figure. Subqueries are primarily used in situations where the criteria for the data being queried are unknown.

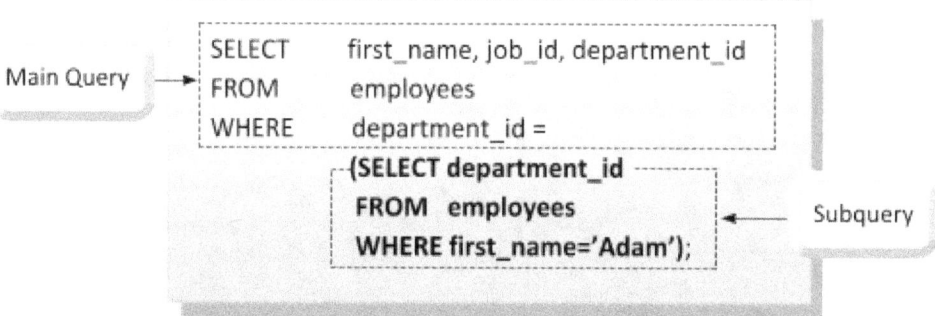

Guidelines

- A **SELECT** statement embedded in a clause of another **SQL** statement is called a subquery.

- A subquery can be placed in the following SQL command clauses: WHERE, HAVING, INTO (a clause of INSERT statement), SET (a clause of UPDATE statement), FROM (a clause used in SELECT and DELETE statements).

- Subqueries must be enclosed in parentheses.

- Subqueries are defined to the right side of the operator.

- Use single row comparison operator (=,>,>=,<,<=,<>) in subqueries that return a single row. For subqueries that return multiple rows, use multi row operators (IN and NOT IN).

- It executes once before the main query, and its result is used to complete the condition defined in the main or outer query.

- Subqueries must not contain the ORDER BY clause, which, if required, should be used in the main SELECT statement.

- You can place any number of subqueries in a single SELECT statement, nested to any level; however, performance must be taken care of while using deep nesting.

Understanding Subquery Process

You will go through a simple example to understand how a subquery, nested in a SELECT statement, is processed. Suppose you want to retrieve names of employees and their respective job ids who are working in the same department as Adam. Keeping in view the existing skills, that you have achieved so far, you will simply pass two separate statements to get the desired result. The first statement would be something like this:

SELECT department_id FROM employees WHERE first_name='Adam';

This statement would return the department number of Adam i.e. 50. Now, to find out other employees working in this department, you would pass the second statement, as follows, to get the required output:

SELECT first_name, job_id FROM employees WHERE department_id=50;

What would you do if you're asked to fetch this result using a single statement, rather than two. The answer is subquery. With the help of a subquery, you can combine the above two statements into one to produce the same result. Here is how it would be done:

SQL Statement

```
SELECT    first_name, job_id, department_id
FROM      employees
WHERE     department_id = (SELECT department_id
                           FROM    employees
                           WHERE   first_name='Adam')
ORDER BY  first_name;
```

In this statement the first query (a subquery) nests into the second one, and is executed first, producing the result: 50. The second query (the main query) is then processed and uses the value (50), returned by the subquery, to complete its WHERE clause.

Note that the subquery used in this example is called a *single row subquery*, because it returned just one row. In such subqueries, you can only use single row comparison operators.

Output

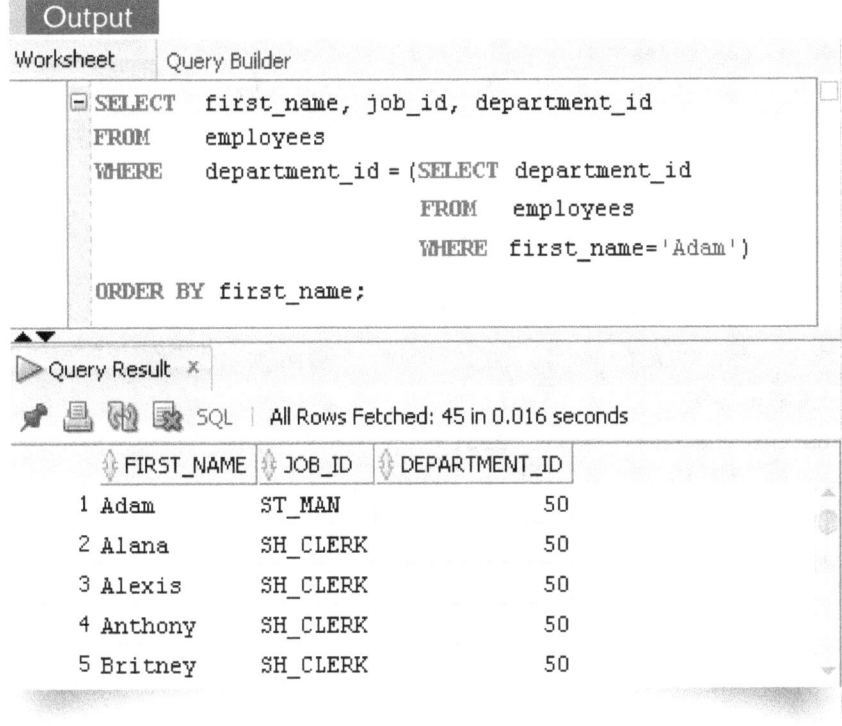

87

Handling Multiple Row Subquery

Subqueries are used to find the data with unknown values, just like the one you used in the previous example to find the department number of Adam together with other information about his colleagues, based on the department number. In that example the subquery returned a single value (the department number of Adam) to process and return the required information. Run the same query for Jennifer. This time you will get an error, saying: *single-row subquery returns more than one row*. The subquery failed because it found two employees with the same first name: Jennifer Dilly in department number 50, and Jennifer Whalen in department number 10. There are two ways to avoid this error. Number one, modify the WHERE clause like this: *WHERE first_name='Jennifer' AND last_name='Dilly'* (if you wish to see the output for department number 50). Number two, use a multiple row comparison operator, such as IN, as demonstrated below. The modified WHERE clause – mentioned in the first recommendation above – would only fetch information of employees working under department 50, while the multiple row comparison operator would also return the sole record of Jennifer Whalen enrolled in department number 10. See record number 16 in the output screenshot.

In this case the subquery returned two departments (10 and 50). In order to handle these multiple values, we used the IN operator, which accepts a list of values. In turn, the main query returned all records for department number 50 (which Jennifer Dilly belongs to), and the sole record of Jeniffer Whalen, who works in department number 10.

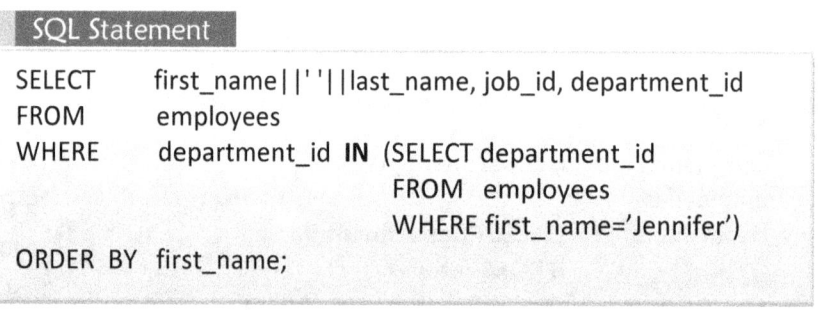

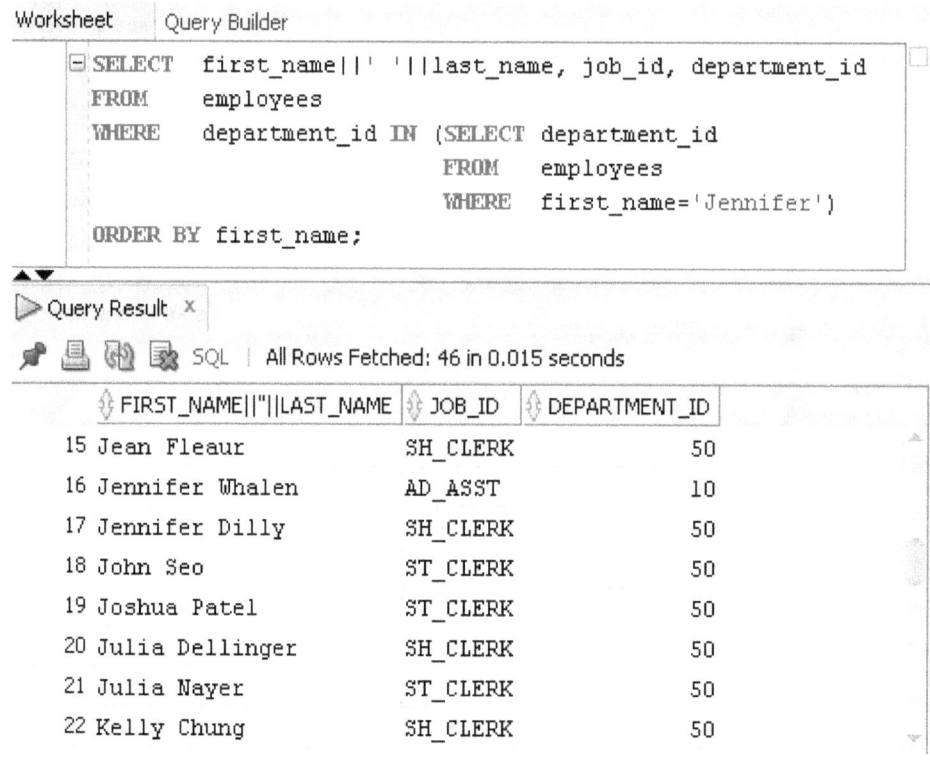

Using Multiple Subqueries in a SELECT Statement

You can define multiple subqueries within a nested query by joining the specified conditions using the AND and OR logical operators. For example, suppose you want to retrieve the names of all employees who have the same job id value as Jennifer Dilly and work in the same department with her. The statement will use two subqueries, joined together using the AND operator, and will be structured as follows. Note that in this statement we used the single row comparison operator (=) to evaluate the job id of Jennifer Dilly, because in the second subquery we eliminated return of multiple rows by specifically mentioning which Jennifer we are referring to. Jennifer Dilly works as shipping clerk (SH_CLERK), so the output will only display her colleagues working as shipping clerk, and will suppress records of two other designations (ST_CLERK – Stock Clerk and ST_MAN – Stock Manager) from her department.

SQL Statement

```
SELECT   first_name||' '||last_name, job_id, department_id
FROM     employees
WHERE    department_id IN (SELECT department_id
                           FROM   employees
                           WHERE  first_name='Jennifer')
         AND job_id = (SELECT job_id
                       FROM   employees
                       WHERE  first_name='Jennifer' AND last_name='Dilly')
ORDER BY first_name;
```

Output

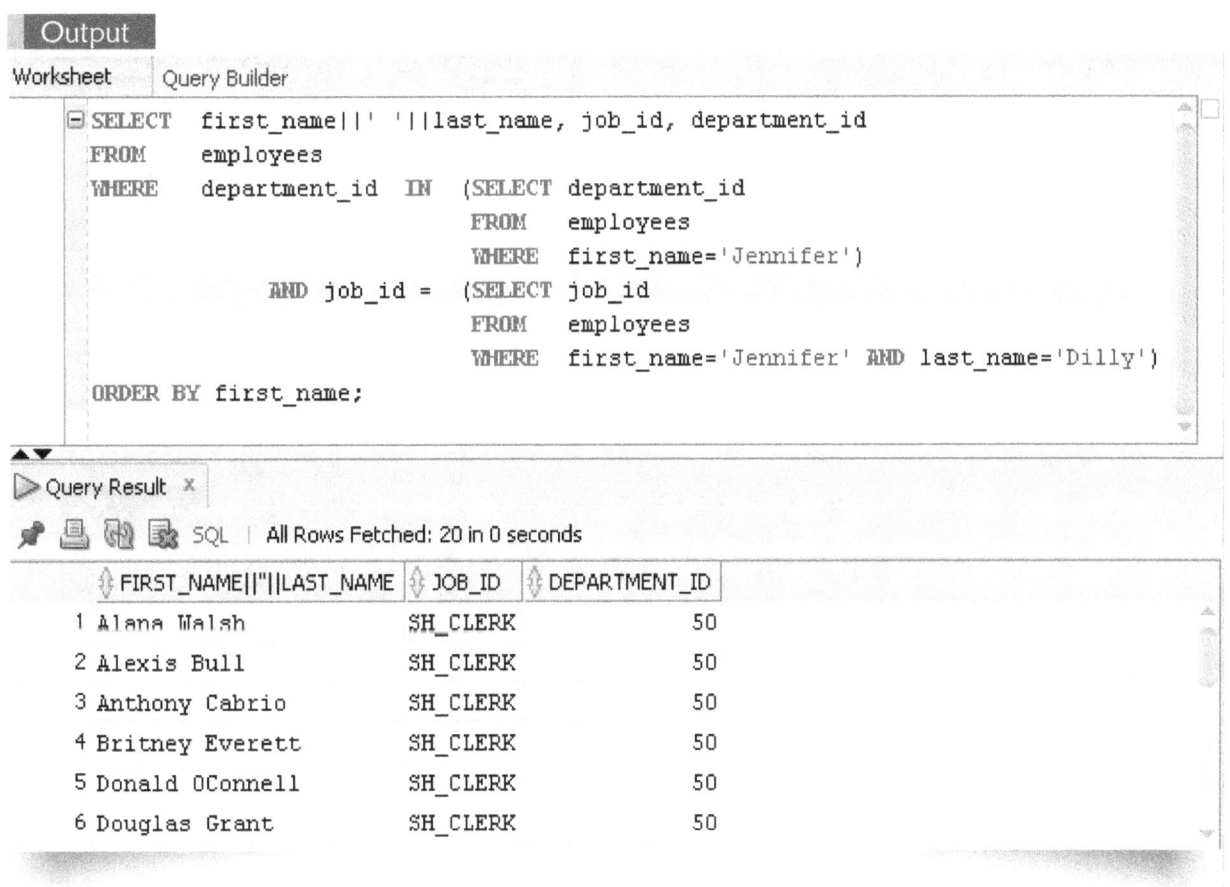

Subquery in the Having Clause

You added subqueries to the WHERE clause in the former two examples. Subqueries can also be used in the HAVING clause. The first query below provides a list of average salaries in each department. It is an auxiliary statement provided to comprehend the result of the second query, which displays all the departments that have an average salary greater than that of department number 80. It is the query which uses a subquery in its HAVING clause. From the first output, you can see that the average salary for department number 80 is 8956. This is the figure which is passed on to the main query to complete the HAVING condition. Consequently, the second output displays the result you intend to see.

SQL Statement

```
SELECT    department_id, round(avg(salary))
FROM      employees
GROUP BY  department_id
ORDER BY  department_id;
```

SQL Statement

```
SELECT    department_id, round(avg(salary))
FROM      employees
GROUP BY  department_id
HAVING    avg(salary) >
          (SELECT avg(salary)
            FROM employees
            WHERE department_id=80)
ORDER BY  department_id;
```

Output

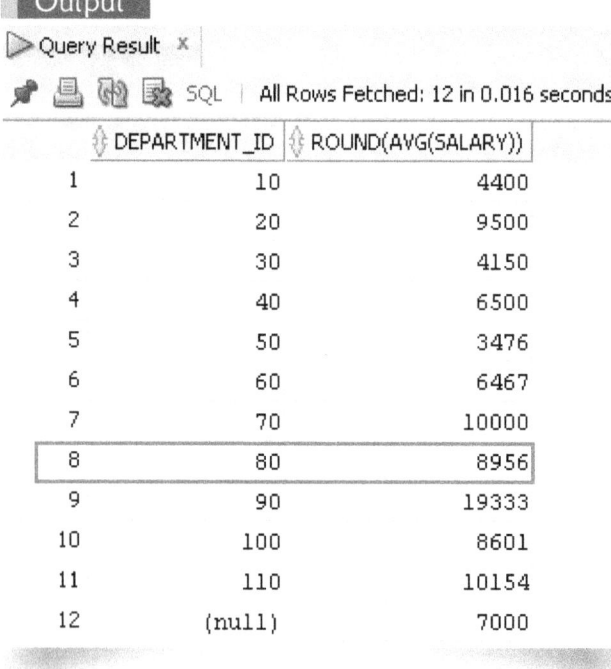

Output

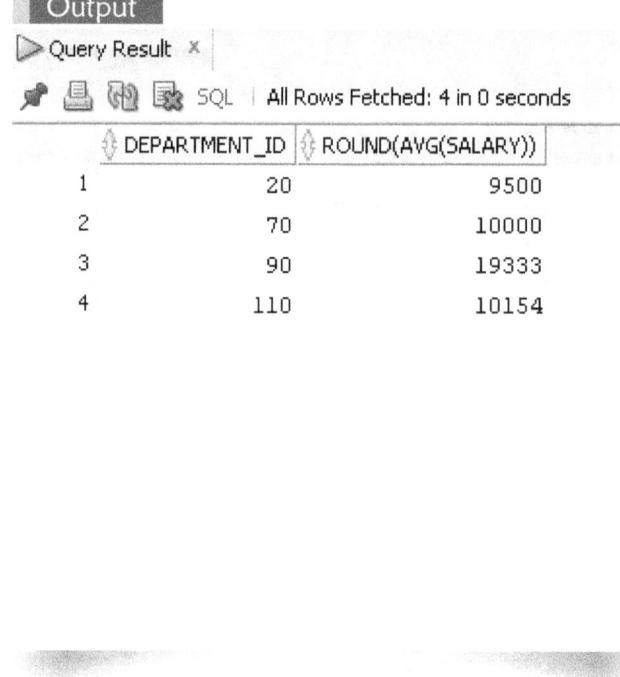

Test Your Skill

1. A subquery can *only* be used in a WHERE clause. Yes / No

2. Identify the two errors in the following statement:

   ```
   SELECT    first_name, job_id, department_id
   FROM      employees
   WHERE     department_id = SELECT department_id
                             FROM   employees
                             WHERE first_name='Adam'
                             ORDER BY department_id;
   ```

3. A subquery which returns multiple rows must use the _____ comparison operator.

    a. Greater than >

    b. Equal to =

    c. LIKE

    d. IN/NOT IN

4. Display name, job id and salary columns for all employees having the same salary as Karen Colmenares.

   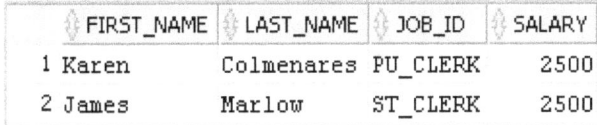

5. Create a query which returns first name, department id, and job title for all employees enrolled under location number 1700 and 2400.

FIRST_NAME	DEPARTMENT_ID	JOB_ID
16 Jennifer	10	AD_ASST
17 Susan	40	HR_REP
18 Shelley	110	AC_MGR

6. Display a list of employees (comprising id, first name, and salary columns) who earn more than the average salary.

	EMPLOYEE_ID	FIRST_NAME	SALARY
1	100	Steven	30000
2	101	Neena	17000

7. Display name and department number of employees who report to Steven King.

	FIRST_NAME	LAST_NAME	DEPARTMENT_ID
2	Lex	De Haan	90
3	Den	Raphaely	30

Query Data From Multiple Tables

Referential Integrity in Relational Databases

All modern DBMSs are also called Relational Database Management Systems (RDBMS), because they all follow a relational database model, which ensures that all of the data in the database is valid according to a set of rules. Referential integrity is also an elemental data integrity rule of the relational database model. Referential integrity defines the relationships among different columns and tables in a relational database. It is called referential integrity because the values in one column or set of columns in a table refers to or must match the values in a related column or set of columns in other tables. For example, the DEPARTMENTS and EMPLOYEES tables in the following figure track different, but related information. The DEPARTMENTS table stores information (such as id, name etc.) about different departments. Each department's record has a unique department ID. The EMPLOYEES table stores employees information along with the department they belong to. EMPLOYEES has a column (DEPARTMENT_ID) to indicate the department of each employee. As you can see, the department ID column in EMPLOYEES refers to the department ID column in DEPARTMENTS. Referential integrity simply makes sure that at all times, whenever a new employee's record is created, it must have a department ID that matches a department ID in the DEPARTMENTS table.

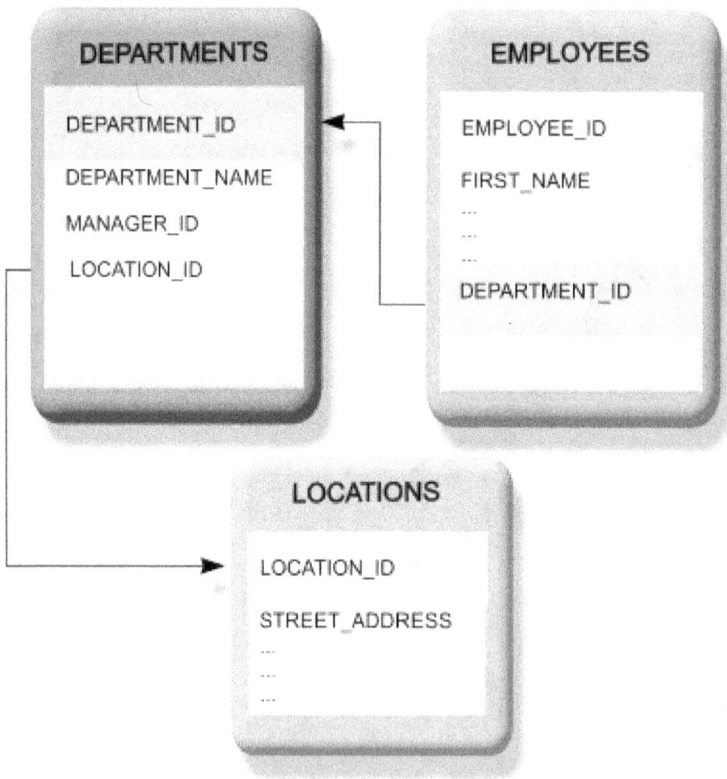

Referential Integrity in Relational Databases

What is a Join?

From the previous discussion it is evident that rows in one table may be joined to rows in another table according to corresponding column values existing in both tables. In database terminology, these columns are referred to as Primary and Foreign key columns, that you already went through in chapter 1.

Whenever you need data from more than one table in the database, you make use of **JOIN**. Join is one of the most important feature in SQL which has the following main types:

1. Equijoin
2. Inner Join
3. Outer Join

Points to Remember:

- Databases performs a join whenever multiple tables appear in the FROM clause of the query.

- The select list of the query can select any columns from any of these tables. The columns in the join conditions need not also appear in the select list.

- If any two of these tables have a column name in common, then you must qualify all references to these columns (by prefixing table names) throughout the query to avoid ambiguity.

- To join tables together, you need a minimum of the number of join conditions summarized as the number of tables minus one. For example, to join four tables, a minimum of three joins would be required.

- As far as SQL is concerned, there is no limit to the number of tables that may be specified in a SELECT statement for creating the join. However, the rules to follow are that all the tables must be listed in the FROM clause, and their relationship is defined in the WHERE clause. Refer to your DBMS documentation which might impose some restrictions on the maximum number of tables per join.

- A WHERE clause that contains a join condition can also contain other conditions that refer to columns of only one table. These conditions can further restrict the rows returned by the join query.

The EQUIJOIN

Equijoin is one of the most commonly used join with a join condition containing an equality operator. It is the most simple join that is used either in the FROM clause or in the WHERE clause of a SELECT statement to show data from multiple related tables. Here is its syntax:

Syntax

```
SELECT   table.column, table.column ...
FROM     table1, table2
WHERE    table1.column = table2.column;
```

NOTE

Using complete table names with qualifying column names can be very time consuming, especially with lengthy table names. You can overcome this problem by using table **aliases** like this:

```
SELECT e.first_name, d.department_name
FROM   employees e, departments d;
```

The following statement is similar to all the previous SELECT statements except for two things. First of all, this statement is now carrying two columns from Employees table and one column from Departments table, as compared to previous examples where all the columns were listed from a single table. Secondly, the FROM clause list two tables. These are the tables that are being joined in the query using the WHERE clause which instructs the DBMS to match department ID in the Employees table with department ID in the Departments table. One more thing that is different from previous examples is the use of table names in the SELECT and WHERE clauses. This expression is called **fully qualified column names** and is used to inform DBMS which department id you are referring to. It is always mandatory to use such qualifiers to avoid ambiguity, which you averted in the following statement due to the presence of the department id column in both tables.

SQL Statement

```
SELECT   employees.first_name, employees.department_id, departments.department_name
FROM     employees, departments
WHERE    employees.department_id=departments.department_id;
```

Output

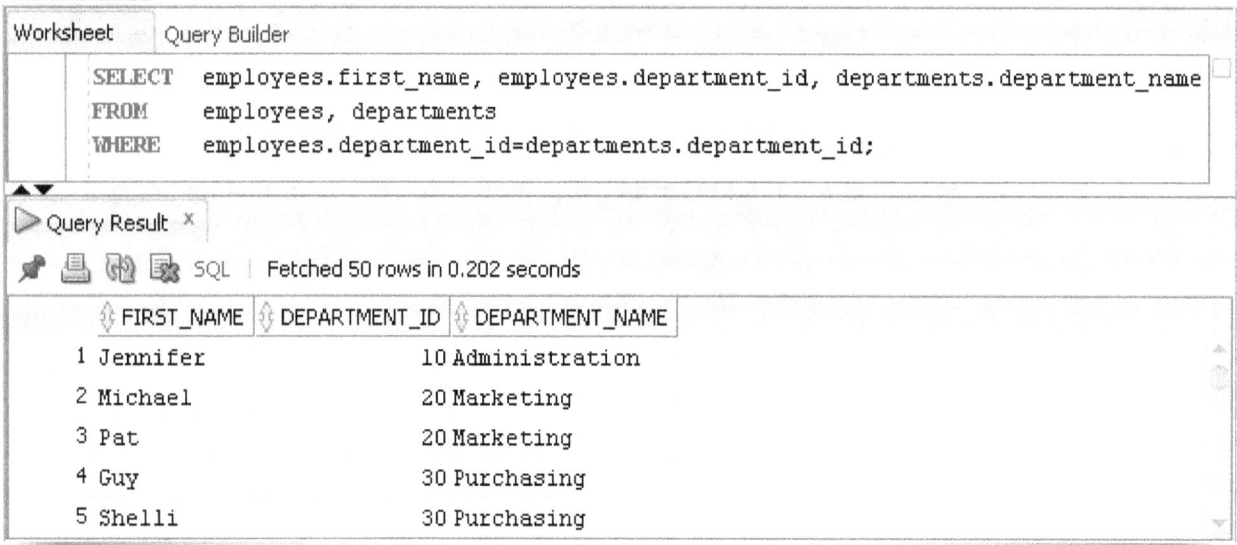

SQL for Everyone

The INNER JOIN

The INNER JOIN is similar to the EQUIJOIN and uses the same equality operator to establish a join between two tables. The difference is that it uses the INNER JOIN keyword in its syntax which explicitly specifies the join. The keyword is used in the FROM clause which makes it different from the previous example. Another difference between the two joins is the use of a special ON clause which is used instead of WHERE to pass the same condition as specified in the WHERE clause previously. You can use both the simple (EQUIJOIN) and the standard (INNER JOIN) syntax formats to produce the same result. However, ANSI SQL standard prefers the INNER JOIN over the simple EQUIJOIN. Depending on your platform, you can use one of the following formats:

Syntax

```
SELECT   table.column, table.column ...
FROM     table1 INNER JOIN table2
ON       table1.column = table2.column;
```

OR

```
SELECT   table.column, table.column ...
FROM     table1 JOIN table2
ON       table1.column = table2.column;
```

The INNER JOIN also returns all rows from the specified tables as long as there is a match between the columns. If there are some rows in the DEPARTMENTS table that do not have matches in EMPLOYEES, these departments will not be fetched. For example, the DEPARTMENTS table has some more department records (120 through 270) that do not have an associated record in the EMPLOYEES table, so these records are eliminated by the INNER JOIN query. See OUTER JOIN in the next section to incorporate these missing departments in the result.

SQL Statement

```
SELECT    D.department_id "ID", D.department_name "Name", E.first_name "Employee"
FROM      departments D INNER JOIN Employees E   ON  D.department_id=E.department_id
ORDER BY  d.department_id;
```

Output

Worksheet | Query Builder

```
SELECT    D.department_id "ID", D.department_name "Name", E.first_name "Employee"
FROM      departments D INNER JOIN Employees E ON D.department_id=E.department_id
ORDER BY  d.department_id;
```

Query Result

SQL | Fetched 50 rows in 0.063 seconds

	ID	Name	Employee
1	10	Administration	Jennifer
2	20	Marketing	Michael
3	20	Marketing	Pat
4	30	Purchasing	Guy
5	30	Purchasing	Shelli

The OUTER JOIN

In the previous two exercises, only those rows were returned by DBMS which satisfied the join condition (e.department_id=d.department_id), and didn't display departments numbering from 120 through 270 because, there were no employees enrolled in these departments. In order to get these missing rows, you are provided with OUTER JOIN operator, which is used in the join condition. Under Oracle implementation, the OUTER JOIN is represented by a plus sign (+) enclosed in parentheses, and is placed on the side of the join that is deficient in information. The operator creates that may NULL rows to which rows from the non-deficient table can be joined, as done in the following example in which all the missing departments are fetched in the output with null values in the Employee column.

Syntax

```
SELECT   table.column, table.column ...
FROM     table1, table2
ON       table1.column = table2.column(+);
```

OR

```
SELECT   table.column, table.column ...
FROM     table1, table2
ON       table1.column(+) = table2.column;
```

SQL Statement

```
SELECT    D.department_id "ID", D.department_name "Name", E.first_name "Employee"
FROM      departments D INNER JOIN Employees E  ON  D.department_id=E.department_id(+)
ORDER BY  d.department_id;
```

Output

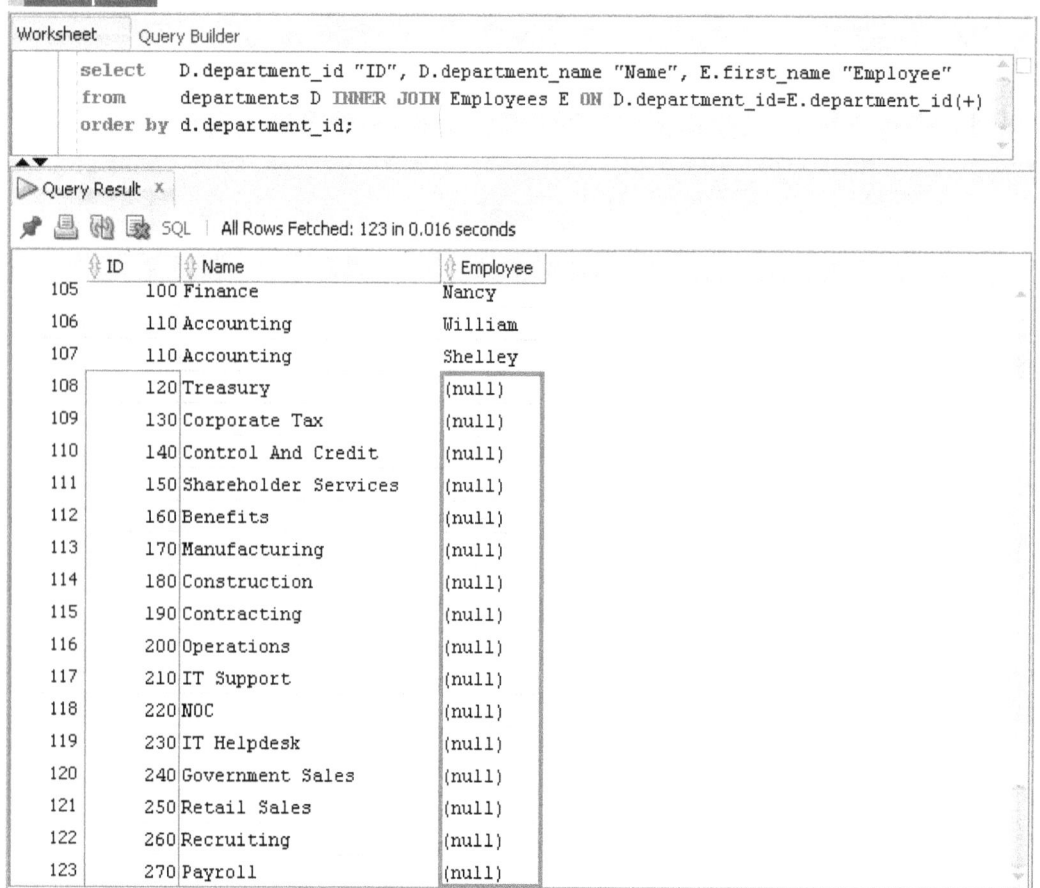

OUTER JOIN (continued)

Some implementations use LEFT JOIN and RIGHT JOIN keywords to create outer joins. The query with the LEFT JOIN get all rows from the left table (table1), with the matching rows in the right table (table2). When there is no match, the right side result displays NULL. The RIGHT JOIN is just the opposite, which displays NULL with no matching rows in the left table. In some implementations, these two are called LEFT OUTER JOIN and RIGHT OUTER JOIN, respectively.

Here is the syntax to use OUTER JOIN for non-Oracle platforms:

Syntax
```
SELECT   table.column, table.column ...
FROM     table1 LEFT JOIN/RIGHT JOIN table2
ON       table1.column = table2.column;
```

> **NOTE**
> In SQLite, there is no RIGHT OUTER JOIN. If you do need this join, simply reverse the order of the tables defined in the FROM and WHERE clauses.

To produce the same output as illustrated on the previous page, you will structure the statement like this:

SQL Statement
```
SELECT   D.department_id, E.employee_id
FROM     departments LEFT OUTER JOIN Employees
ON       department.department_id = employees.employee_id;
```

JOINS vs. SUBQUERIES

The data that you retrieve using joins can also be retrieved through subqueries. The question arises that which one is better? From technical point of view you must use joins when you can retrieve the same information using either a query that joins multiple tables or a query that has one or more subqueries. In some situations you might use nested subqueries, spreading multiple levels, to get the desired information. However, as a general rule, nested queries or queries with nested subqueries execute slower than queries that join multiple table. So, you should probably not use nested queries unless you cannot retrieve the desired result using joins.

Test Your Skill

1. Which integrity constraint would you enforce to create a joint statement:
   a. Entity
   b. Referential
   c. Column
   d. User Defined

2. The columns in the join condition must also exist in the SELECT list. Yes / No

3. You can select a column from a table not used in the FROM clause. Yes / No

4. What would you do if two tables in a join query have a common column name.

5. How many conditions will you add to a query which uses five tables.

6. Create a query which displays name of employees with their department names as follows:

   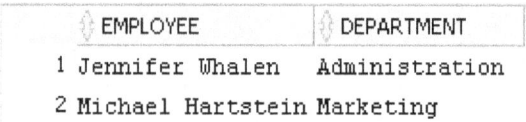

7. Write a query to display the name of employees and department names for John.

   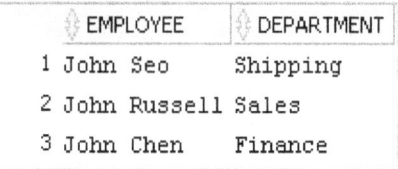

8. Form a statement which shows the first name, department name, and city (from the Locations table) of all employees who earn a commission.

   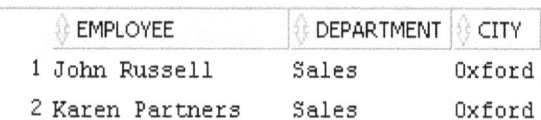

9. Form a statement by joining Countries and Locations tables to display the following output. Use the OUTERJOIN operator to find missing countries in the Locations table.

   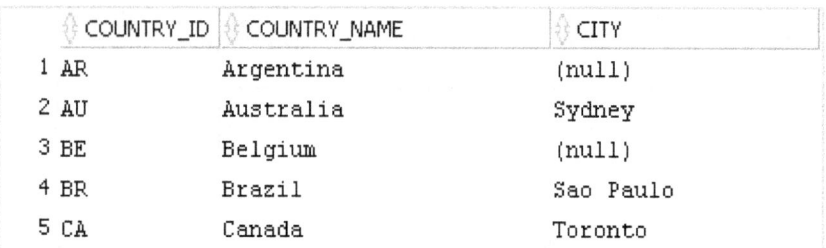

Creating Tables

7

Chapter 7 – Creating Tables

What is a Table?

A table is the basic object in a database which is created to store data. Each table in a database contains information for a particular category. For example, the Employees table, which you have been using so far, contains a list of employees along with other specific information about each employee. A database can have multiple tables to store information about each category separately. For instance, Departments is another table in the database which contains specific information about each department. Besides being separate, tables can also relate to each other using specific keys, known as primary and foreign keys. For example, the Employees table relates to the Departments table using the department id column. This column is created as a foreign key in the Employees table, which references a column with the same name in the Departments table, where it acts as a primary key. This kind of relationship helps in retrieving data from multiple tables (using Joins), as you saw in the previous chapter.

A table is the basic unit of data organization in a database. Each table has its own definition which comprises a table name and set of columns. A column identifies an attribute of the entity described by the table. For example, the column employee_id in the Employees table refers to the employee ID attribute of an employee entity. When you create a table, you specify columns that the table will carry and provide a name to each column, define data type for each column, and a width. You must specify a data type for each column in the table. Values subsequently inserted in a column assume the column data type. For example, the data type for employee_id is NUMBER(6), indicating that this column can only contain numeric data up to 6 digits in width. The width can be predetermined by the data type, as with DATE. After creating a table, you can insert, update, delete, and query rows using SQL. A row is a collection of column information corresponding to a record in a table. For example, a row in the employees table describes the attributes of a specific employee. The following figure illustrates the definition of the Employees table, along with rows in it.

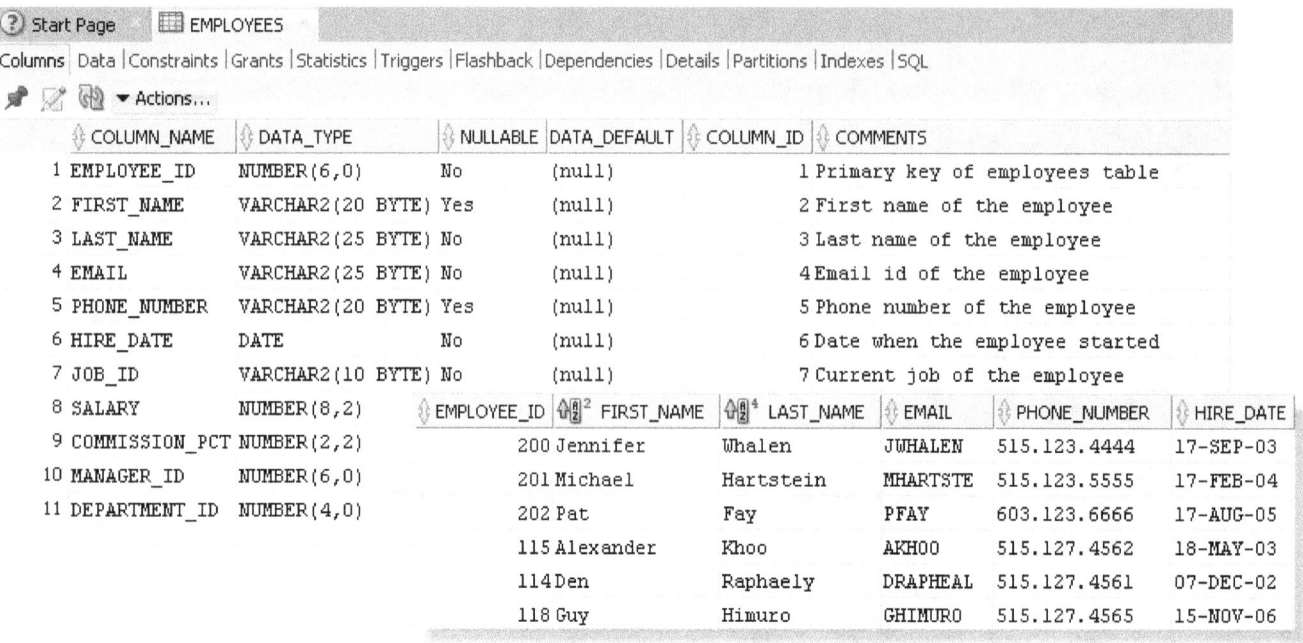

This chapter is dedicated to handling tables, but first, you must acquaint yourself with data types which are declared for each column during the table creation process.

What are Data Types?

Each value that you store in database tables has a data type which associates a fixed set of properties with the value. These properties cause database to treat values of one data type differently from values of another. When a table is created, all of its column are specified with respective data types. These data types define the domain of values that each column can contain. For example, DATE columns cannot accept the value 'RIAZ' or the values 5 or 31 November. Similarly, a number column too doesn't accept character values in it.

Just like many other differences found among different implementations, data types also vary from one DBMS to the next. Even the name of a data type in one DBMS can mean different things to others. Again, you are recommended to go through your DBMS documentations for details on its supported data types.

Another important thing that you must take care of when designing tables is the use of proper data types. You can suffer severe consequences in the future if you select wrong data types. Although you can change data types afterward, it is a real deadly task which can also cause loss of data.

The table that follows lists some of the most common data types that you will experiment with as a beginner.

DATA TYPE	DESCRIPTION
CHAR(size)	It stores fixed-length character data of length *size* characters. For example, the country id column, in the Country table residing in the database you are connected to, is defined as Char(2), which means that you cannot enter more than two characters in this column. In Oracle, the maximum size of this data type is 2000 characters. Default and minimum size is 1 character.
VARCHAR2(size)	This data type is used to store character strings of variable length. In some implementations it is defined as VARCHAR. In Oracle, you must specify a size for this data type, where its maximum size is 4000 characters, and minimum is 1 character.
NUMBER [(p [, s])]	As the name suggests, this one stores numbers having precision *p* and scale *s*. In Oracle, the precision *p* can range from 1 to 38, while the scale *s* can range from -84 to 127. Its default size is 38. There are some more numeric data types supported by other DBMSs e.g. Decimal, Int (small for Integer), Real, Money, Currency, and so on.
DATE	Used to store dates, this data type ranges from January 1, 4712 BC, to December 31, 9999 AD, and contains the datetime elements YEAR, MONTH, DAY, HOUR, MINUTE, and SECOND.
BLOB	A BLOB (Binary Large Object) is a data type that can hold large amount of data. BLOBs are handy for storing digitized information (e.g. images, audios, and videos).

> **NOTE** The CHAR and VARCHAR types are similar, but differ in the way they are stored and retrieved. CHAR data type accepts a fixed number of characters, whereas VARCHAR2 accepts text of any variable length (the maximum varies by DBMS). So, if the string 'Riaz Ahmed' is stored in a column specified as CHAR(25), a full 30 characters are stored, and the text is padded with spaces. In VARCHAR2 only the data specified is saved and no extra data is stored. If you assign a value to a CHAR or VARCHAR2 column that exceeds the column's maximum length, the value is truncated.

How to Create Tables?

Tables in a database are created by issuing CREATE TABLE command, which is one of the data definition language (DDL) command. To remind you, DDL commands are a subset of SQL commands used to create, modify, and remove database objects. This command has a very long syntax; however, here is the short and simple version to begin with.

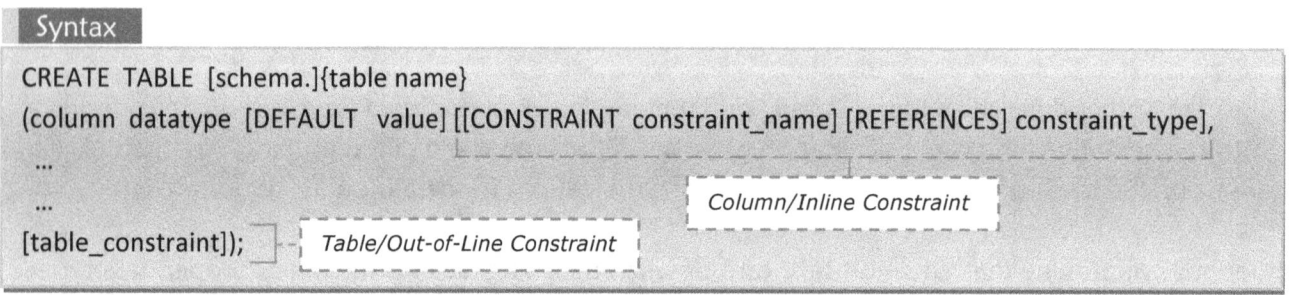

Where:

Schema	A schema is a logical place in the database where you place new tables. It is an optional clause in this syntax. By default, the table is created in the schema you are currently connected to.
Table Name	It is a mandatory clause where you define a name for the new table. Follow the rules outlined below for naming database tables: • Start table and column names with an alphabetic character (A-Z or a-z). • The name can be 1-30 characters long. • Names must contain only alphabets (A-Z or a-z), numbers (0-9), or three special characters(_[underscore], $ and #). • Table name must not duplicate the name of another table in the same schema. Similarly, columns in the same table must not use the same name. However, columns in different tables can share the same name, and the same table name can be used in other schemas. • Never use database reserve words (SELECT, USER etc.) to name tables. • Use the same column entity in different tables for easy referencing. For example, the department number column is named DEPARTMENT_ID in Departments, Employees, and Job History tables. • Table and column names are case-insensitive i.e. EMPLOYEES is treated as employees, which is the same as Employees.
Column	is the name of the column. Follow the instructions provided above for table naming.
Data Type	is the data type of the column with the desired length.
DEFAULT value	is an optional clause, which defines a default value for a column. The defined value gets added to the table when the corresponding column's value is omitted at the time of record creation.
Constraint	Constraints are usually defined while creating a table and can be put either at column or table level. More details about constraints are provided in the next section.

What are Constraints?

We discussed referential integrity in the previous chapter. It is a mechanism in which keys are used to create references among database tables. To keep your database in a consistent state, you need a process which ensure that only valid data gets into the underlying tables. This process is implemented by means of **integrity constraints** – rules that restricts values in a database. Constraints are imposed on tables to enforce referential integrity to prevent loss of data consistency. The following table presents some major constraint types, supported by all major DBMSs. Note that the constraints are usually defined when tables are created. If needed, you can also enforce them at a later stage; however, the recommended way is to plan and implement them at an early stage, prior to inserting data in relevant tables.

The two major advantages of implementing constraints are:

- They enforce rules at the table level whenever a record is inserted, updated, or deleted. In order to execute these three operations successfully, the defined constraint(s) must be satisfied.
- Prevents deletion of table and records if there exist dependent tables and records. Such constraints are useful to eliminate chances of accidental deletions.

Most databases let you create the following five types of constraints and let you declare them syntactically in two ways.

- As part of the definition of an individual column. This is called inline specification.
- As part of the table definition. This is called out-of-line specification.

CONSTRAINT	DESCRIPTION
NOT NULL	Prohibits a table column value from being null. Columns without the NOT NULL constraint can contain null values by default. NOT NULL constraints must be declared **inline**. All other constraints can be declared either inline or out of line. The first example below creates a NOT NULL constraint for the phone number column, without specifying a constraint name. *CREATE TABLE Employees (…, phone_number varchar2(20)* **NOT NULL**, *…);* In the following example, the NOT NULL constraint is applied to the first name column. In this case, an expressive constraint name (emp_fname_nn) is provided, which stands for *employee first name not null*. Providing meaningful names to constraints help in easy future referencing. *CREATE TABLE Employees* *(…, first_name varchar2(20)* **CONSTRAINT emp_fname_nn** *NOT NULL, …);*

CONSTRAINT	DESCRIPTION
UNIQUE	It prohibits multiple rows from having the same value in the same column, and allows null values if it is based on a single column. You can also create composite unique key which designates a combination of columns as the unique key. Use the UNIQUE keyword when you define this constraint inline. You must also specify one or more columns when it is defined as out of line constraint. You must define a composite unique key out of line. You cannot designate the same column or combination of columns as both a primary key and a unique key. The phone number column in the Employees table is a good candidate for this constraint, because every employee has a unique phone number. By making this column unique you can avoid duplicate values that might arise from typos. The following sample shows how to define an inline UNIQUE constraint. *CREATE TABLE Employees* *(…, phone_number varchar2(20)* **CONSTRAINT emp_phone_uk UNIQUE***, …);* The following example defines an out of line composite unique key on the combination of the employee_id and phone_number columns. The emp_id_phone_uk constraint ensures that the same combination of employee id and phone number values does not appear in the table twice. *CREATE TABLE Employees* *(employee_id number(6), …, phone_number varchar2(20), hire_date date, …,* *CONSTRAINT emp_id_phone_uk UNIQUE (employee_id, phone_number));* At first glance the UNIQUE constraint looks similar to the Primary Key constraint, but it is not the same as or synonymous to a PRIMARY KEY constraint. It differs from a primary key in the following ways: • You can define multiple UNIQUE keys in a table, but a table can have one and only one PRIMARY KEY. • Columns defined as UNIQUE constraints can have NULL values; PRIMARY KEY columns can't. • A PRIMARY KEY can be defined as a Foreign Key in other tables; such a relationship cannot be created for UNIQUE keys. • You can modify values in a UNIQUE key in a table as compared to values stored in a PRIMARY KEY which are not modifiable.

SQL for Everyone

CONSTRAINT	DESCRIPTION
PRIMARY KEY	Uniquely identified each row in a table. You use it to combine the above two constraints in a single declaration. A primary key cannot be null and must not allow duplicates. This constraint is basically applied to ensure that other DML operations (such as UPDATE and DELETE) execute successfully. In the absence of a Primary Key, these two commands would never know which rows a user intend to manipulate. Primary Key constraints can be defined inline or out of line. A composite Primary Key must be defined out of line. See Chapter 1 for more details on primary keys. A Primary Key constraint is usually defined inline when it is based on just one column, as shown here: CREATE TABLE Employees (employee_id number(6) CONSTRAINT emp_id_pk PRIMARY KEY, ...); If it is based on multiple columns, then you must define this constraint out of line, like the one that follows. This constraint, which is called Composite Primary Key, ensures that an employee is not enrolled again in the same department. CREATE TABLE Employees (employee_id number(6), ..., department_id number(4), CONSTRAINT emp_id_pk PRIMARY KEY (employee_id, department_id));

CONSTRAINT	DESCRIPTION
FOREIGN KEY	The FOREIGN KEY constraint designates a column or set of columns as a foreign key. It is created to establish and enforce relationships among tables. Also see Chapter 1 for more details on Foreign Keys. Remember the following key points related to FOREIGN KEYS: • The table containing the foreign key is called the child table, and the table containing the referenced key is called the parent table. A foreign key value must match an existing value in the parent table. • Columns of the foreign key and the referenced key must match in order and data type. • You can define a foreign key constraint on a single key column either inline or out of line; a composite foreign key must be specified on out of line attribute. • You can define multiple foreign keys in a table. Also, a single column can be part of more than one foreign key. • Since no part of a primary key can be null, therefore, a foreign key that is part of a primary key cannot be null as well. The following clauses are used when you define foreign key constraints: **FOREIGN KEY** This keyword is used only when you define the constraint out of line. **REFERENCES** It is used with both inline and out of line declaration to identify the parent table and its column(s). **ON DELETE CASCADE** Besides enforcing referential integrity, foreign keys are defined to prevent accidental deletion of records from the parent table(s). For example, you cannot delete a department which has employees. Such a department's record can be deleted either by deleting records of all the employees enrolled under it, or by using the ON DELETE CASCADE option. It is used when you want to remove a parent record along with all child records at once. Without this option, the row in the parent table cannot be deleted if it is referenced in the child table. *Continued ...* →

SQL for Everyone

CONSTRAINT	DESCRIPTION
FOREIGN KEY *(continued)*	The following statement defines a foreign key on the department_id column that references the primary key on the department_id column in the Departments table: *CREATE TABLE Employee* *(employee_id number(4), ...,* *department_id CONSTRAINT emp_deptno_fk REFERENCES Departments(department_id));* The constraint emp_deptno_fk ensures that a department given to an employee in the Employees table is present in the Departments table. However, employees can have null department numbers, meaning that they do not relate to any department. If provision of department is mandatory, then you could create a NOT NULL constraint on the department_id column in the Employees table in addition to the REFERENCES constraint. Also note that the above example didn't use the FOREIGN KEY clause, because the constraint was defined inline. Moreover, in Oracle, the data type of the department_id column is not needed as well, because it is done automatically by Oracle using the data type of the referenced key. The following statement defines this foreign key constraint out of line: *CREATE TABLE Employee* *(employee_id number(4), ...,* *department_id, CONSTRAINT emp_deptno_fk FOREIGN KEY (department_id) REFERENCES Departments(department_id));* Both these variations of the foreign key constraint omitted the ON DELETE CASCADE clause, instructing DBMS to not delete a department if an employee is associated with it.

CONSTRAINT	DESCRIPTION

CHECK	It is applied on table columns to ensure that the value being stored complies with the specified condition. The CHECK constraint uses the same syntax for both inline and out-of-line attributes. However, inline specification can refer only to the column currently being defined, whereas out-of-line specification can refer to multiple columns.
	
	The following statement creates a table and defines a check constraint in each column of the table:
	
	CREATE TABLE departments
	(department_id NUMBER CONSTRAINT dept_no_chk
	    CHECK (department_id BETWEEN 10 AND 99),
	department_name VARCHAR2(30) CONSTRAINT dept_name_chk
	    CHECK (department_name = UPPER(department_name)),
	location VARCHAR2(10) CONSTRAINT dept_loc_chk
	    CHECK (location IN ('SEATTLE','TORONTO','TOKYO','LONDON')));
	
	The purpose of all the three constraints defined in the above table is to restrict the values in respective columns.
	
	dept_no_chk ensures that no department numbers are less than 10 or greater than 99.
	dept_name_chk ensures that all division names are in uppercase.
	dept_loc_chk restricts locations to Seattle, Toronto, Tokyo, or London.
	
	The following statement creates a table with an out of line check constraint:
	
	CREATE TABLE employees
	(..., salary NUMBER(8,2), commission_pct NUMBER(5,2), ...,
	CONSTRAINT emp_sal_chk CHECK (salary * commission_pct <= 5000));
	
	The emp_sal_chk constraint implements a condition which puts an upper cap of 5000 to limit total commission of each employee by comparing the product of salary and commission percent with the defined upper limit. If you enter a new record in this table with some values for both salary and commission, then the product of these values must not exceed 5000 in order to comply with the constraint. On the other hand, if any of these columns has a null value, then the product of the calculation is also null which automatically satisfies the constraint.

Create a Table

By now I assume that not only you have grasped the basic concepts about constraints, but have also become familiar with the use of CREATE TABLE command. To complete the exercise, let's create a table and implement all the five constraints in it.

SQL Statement

```
CREATE TABLE department_clone
(
  department_id     number(4)  CONSTRAINT pk_dept_id PRIMARY KEY,
  department_name   varchar2(3) CONSTRAINT nn_dept_name NOT NULL,
  location_id       number(4)  CONSTRAINT fk_dept_loc REFERENCES locations (location_id),
  CONSTRAINT uk_dept_name_loc UNIQUE (department_name, location_id)
);
```

Explanation

CONSTRAINT	EXPLANATION
PK_DEPT_ID	This is an **inline constraint** which identifies the department id column as the **primary key** of the department_clone table. By defining this constraint, you eliminated the chances of having the same number for two different departments, and also declared that this column must not accept NULL values.
NN_DEPT_NAME	This is also an **inline constraint**, defined to implement the **NOT NULL** constraint. It ensures that each department in the table must have a name.
FK_DEPT_LOC	This **inline constraint** is created to implement **foreign key** constraint. It guarantees that any location id entered in this table must already exist in the Locations table. Note that before defining this foreign key constraint the Locations table must exist, with a primary key constraint on the id column, prior to executing this entire CREATE statement.
UK_DEPT_NAME_LOC	It's a **unique key** constraint defined as **out-of-line**. It uses two columns from the table to form a composite unique key to ensure that the same combination of department name and location id doesn't appear in the table again.

Chapter 7 – Creating Tables

Create Table From Another Table

A situation has surfaced that demands you to create a new table based on an existing one. Not only must you create the new table with the same structure, but you must also incorporate all the records from the existing table into the new one. Does SQL provides a solution to cope with this scenario? In fact, yes, it does. It is an alternate method to creating a table in which you use a subquery with the AS clause of the CREATE TABLE command to both create the table and insert rows into it. Here is its syntax:

Syntax

```
CREATE TABLE {table name}
[(column specification, column specification, ...)]
{AS subquery};
```

Let's go through some examples to understand the above syntax.

CREATE TABLE emp2 AS SELECT * FROM Employees;

The above statement creates an exact copy of the Employees table. It creates the new table (emp2) with the same structure and populates it with all records from the source table. Note that this example didn't use the optional column specification clause. When no column specifications are provided, then the column names of the target table are the same as the column names in the source table. Also note that no integrity constraints associated with the source table are inherited to the target table.

CREATE TABLE emp3 (id, name, hiredate) AS SELECT employee_id,first_name,hire_date FROM Employees;

In this statement the new table is created using some specific columns from the source table. In this type of table creation you can set names for the column in the target table different from the source columns, but the number of new columns must equal the number of columns in the subquery SELECT list.

CREATE TABLE emp4 AS SELECT * FROM Employees WHERE department_id=50;

Here, you created a new table using all columns (*) from the source table, just like the first statement above. It differs from the previous one in the way that, it uses the WHERE clause to limit the record insertion in accordance with the specified condition, which instructs to only insert records of employees working in department number 50.

> **NOTE**
> Since the subquery is based on the SELECT statement, you can use other clauses of this command as well, including WHERE and GROUP BY. You can also use joins in the subquery to insert data from multiple tables. Irrespective of the number of the source tables defined in the FROM clause, data will only be fetched into a single table.

SQL for Everyone

Alter Table

After creating a table you realized that something went wrong with it creation and you need to change its definition. After creating a table you can modify its structure by using ALTER TABLE command. It is a data definition command (DDL) which allows you to:

- Add a new column to the table
- Modify column width
- Delete a column from the table
- Rename a column
- Rename tables
- Add/drop constraints
- Enable/disable constraints
- Rename constraints

> **NOTE**
> Take special care while using DDL commands as these command are irreversible. Once executed, you cannot roll them back.

Add Column

Let's start the proceedings by adding a new column to a table which you can do using the ADD clause of the ALTER TABLE command. The ALTER TABLE command's syntax is very similar to CREATE TABLE with the exception of three clauses (ADD, MODIFY and DROP), as shown below. This exercise assumes that you already have emp2 table, which you created on the previous page.

Syntax

```
ALTER TABLE {table name}
ADD ({column datatype [DEFAULT value] [constraint specification]}[, column ... , ...]
    );
```

SQL Statement

```
ALTER TABLE emp2
ADD (ss_number char(9) CONSTRAINT emp_phone_uk UNIQUE );
```

In the above statement, you added a new column to record social security numbers of employees. Since this number has a fixed format, we used the CHAR data type. Each employee has a unique social security number, therefore, we created a UNIQUE constraint for this column, to eliminate duplicate values. Also note that we intentionally provided a wrong constraint name (emp_phone_uk), which will be dropped in a subsequent section.

Chapter 7 – Creating Tables

Modify Column

After adding the social security column to the Employees table, you realized that you made couple of mistakes in the ALTER TABLE statement as well. First, you should have set the size of this column to 11 instead of 9 to save the number in 999-99-9999 format – including the two dashes. Secondly, the name of the unique constraint was also wrong. In the following statement, you'll resolve the first issue by resizing the column width using the MODIFY clause of the command. Always keep the following guidelines in mind when you modify column definitions:

- Decrease the width of a column only when it contains null values.
- Change the data type if there are no values in the column.
- The DEFAULT value takes effect for subsequent insertions.
- Use the NOT NULL constraint only when there are no values.

Syntax

```
ALTER TABLE {table name}
MODIFY {(column datatype [DEFAULT value] }[, column ... , ...]
       );
```

SQL Statement

ALTER TABLE emp2 **MODIFY** (ss_number char(11));

Output

COLUMN_NAME	DATA_TYPE
EMPLOYEE_ID	NUMBER(6,0)
FIRST_NAME	VARCHAR2(20 BYTE)
LAST_NAME	VARCHAR2(25 BYTE)
EMAIL	VARCHAR2(25 BYTE)
PHONE_NUMBER	VARCHAR2(20 BYTE)
HIRE_DATE	DATE
JOB_ID	VARCHAR2(10 BYTE)
SALARY	NUMBER(8,2)
COMMISSION_PCT	NUMBER(2,2)
MANAGER_ID	NUMBER(6,0)
DEPARTMENT_ID	NUMBER(4,0)
SS_NUMBER	CHAR(11 BYTE)

Delete Column

You are also allowed to drop columns from a table provided that they do not contain values. The syntax here shows the two flavors of this clause. Use the first one if you want to drop a single column. For this scenario, the COLUMN keyword must follow the DROP clause, followed by the column name. Apply the second one if you need to drop multiple columns. For this, use the DROP clause only, followed by a list of columns enclosed in parentheses, and separated by commas.

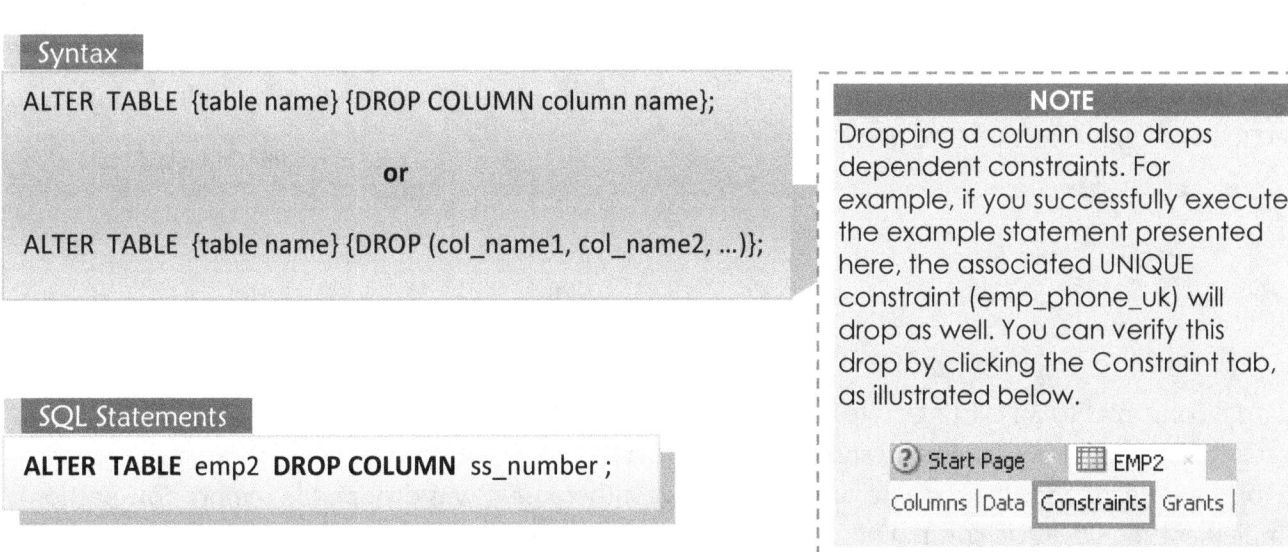

Syntax

ALTER TABLE {table name} {DROP COLUMN column name};

or

ALTER TABLE {table name} {DROP (col_name1, col_name2, ...)};

NOTE
Dropping a column also drops dependent constraints. For example, if you successfully execute the example statement presented here, the associated UNIQUE constraint (emp_phone_uk) will drop as well. You can verify this drop by clicking the Constraint tab, as illustrated below.

SQL Statements

ALTER TABLE emp2 **DROP COLUMN** ss_number ;

Rename Column

After creating a table you can change the name of its columns considering the following restrictions.

- The new name must not conflict with the name of any existing column in the table.
- Dependent views, triggers, functions, and procedures can become invalid, and you may need to alter these objects with the new column name.

The following example renames the salary column of the emp2 table to monthly_salary.

Syntax

ALTER TABLE {table name}
RENAME COLUMN {old column TO new column};

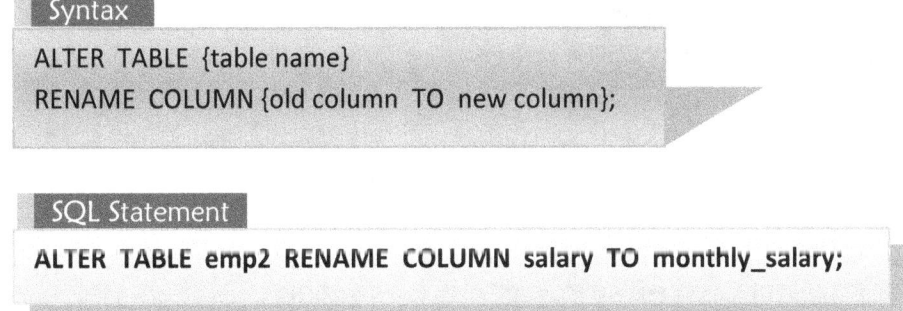

SQL Statement

ALTER TABLE emp2 RENAME COLUMN salary TO monthly_salary;

Chapter 7 – Creating Tables

Renaming Table

Use the RENAME TO clause of the ALTER TABLE command to change the name of an existing table. The following statement renames an existing table emp4 to emp5.

Syntax

    ALTER TABLE previous table name RENAME TO new table name;

SQL Statement

    ALTER TABLE emp4 RENAME TO emp5;

> **NOTE**
> In Microsoft SQL Server execute the sp_rename procedure to change the name of a table. The following example renames the test1 table to test2 in the HR schema.
>
> EXEC sp_rename 'hr.test1', 'test2';
> GO

Add Constraint After Creating a Table

To add a constraint to an existing table you use the ADD CONSTRAINT clause of the ALTER TABLE command. The following statements show how to add all the four constraints to a table after its creation. The third statement adds the social security column again (because it was dropped in the previous section), to implement the UNIQUE constraint.

Syntax

    ALTER TABLE {table name}
    {ADD CONSTRAINT [constraint name] {constraint type (column | expression)};

SQL Statements

    ALTER TABLE emp2 ADD CONSTRAINT pk_emp2_id PRIMARY KEY (employee_id) ;
    ALTER TABLE emp2 ADD CONSTRAINT fk_emp2_dept_id FOREIGN KEY (department_id)
                                    REFERENCES Departments(department_id);
    ALTER TABLE emp2 ADD (ss_number char(11)); -- recreated the SS number column
    ALTER TABLE emp2 ADD CONSTRAINT uk_emp2_ss_number UNIQUE (ss_number) ;
    ALTER TABLE emp2 ADD CONSTRAINT ck_emp2_salary CHECK (salary > 0);

> **NOTE**
> SQLite only supports RENAME TABLE and ADD COLUMN clauses of the ALTER TABLE command. Other variants, such as DROP COLUMN, ADD and DROP CONSTRAINT are not supported by this DBMS. To correct a table, you will have to create a new table with proper definitions, transfer the data (using INSERT INTO command) from the old table, drop the old table, and rename the new table as the old one. This solution is applicable to simple databases; however, you'll have to do much more to handle a complex database.

Drop Constraint

Use the DROP clause of the ALTER TABLE command to remove a constraint. Its syntax contains the following sub-clauses:

- **PRIMARY KEY** Use the PRIMARY KEY keyword to drop the primary key constraint of a table.
- **UNIQUE** Specify UNIQUE to drop the unique constraint on the specified columns.
- **CONSTRAINT** If the constraint being dropped is neither a Primary Key nor a Unique key, then use the CONSTRAINT clause followed by the constraint name to drop an integrity constraint.
- **CASCADE** The CASCADE option causes any dependent constraints also to be dropped. You cannot drop a primary key or unique key constraint that is part of a referential integrity constraint without also dropping the foreign key. To drop the referenced key and the foreign key together, use the CASCADE clause.

Syntax

```
ALTER TABLE {table name}
DROP  PRIMARY KEY | UNIQUE (column) | CONSTRAINT constraint name [CASCADE];
```

SQL Statements

```
CREATE TABLE dept2 AS SELECT * FROM Departments;
CREATE TABLE emp4  AS SELECT * FROM Employees;

ALTER TABLE dept2 ADD CONSTRAINT  pk_dept2_id PRIMARY KEY (department_id) ;
ALTER TABLE emp4  ADD CONSTRAINT  pk_emp4_id PRIMARY KEY (employee_id) ;
ALTER TABLE emp4  ADD CONSTRAINT  fk_emp4_dept_id FOREIGN KEY (department_id)
                                  REFERENCES dept2(department_id);
```

ALTER TABLE dept2 **DROP PRIMARY KEY CASCADE**;
The above statement removes the primary key constraint on the dept2 table and drops the associated foreign key constraint (fk_emp4_dept_id) defined on the department_id column in the emp4 table.

ALTER TABLE emp2 **DROP UNIQUE**(ss_number);
To drop a unique constraint use the UNIQUE keyword followed by the column name. The constraint was added to the table on the previous page.

ALTER TABLE emp2 **DROP CONSTRAINT** fk_emp2_dept_id;
This one drops the foreign key constraint which was created on the previous page. Use the CONSTRAINT clause to drop an integrity constraint other than a primary key or unique constraint.

Enable/Disable Constraint

In situations where you want to block an existing constraint temporarily without permanently dropping it, you can use the ENABLE/DISABLE clauses of the ALTER TABLE command. The DISABLE clause deactivates an integrity constraint, and applying the CASCADE option with it disables dependent constraints as well. Once you're out of the situation, simply turn the constraint back on using the ENABLE clause. These two clauses can be used in both the CREATE and ALTER table commands.

Syntax

```
ALTER TABLE {table name}
DISABLE | ENABLE CONSTRAINT constraint name [CASCADE];
```

SQL Statements

```
ALTER TABLE emp2 DISABLE CONSTRAINT ck_emp2_salary;   -- constraint deactivated

ALTER TABLE emp2 ENABLE CONSTRAINT ck_emp2_salary;    -- constraint activated
```

Renaming Constraint

The RENAME CONSTRAINT clause of the ALTER TABLE command lets you rename any existing constraint. Note that you cannot use the name of an existing constraint in the same schema. Renaming a constraint has no impact on the dependent objects which remain valid. The following statement renames the old constraint name (ck_emp2_salary) on the emp2 table to ck_emp2_min_salary.

Syntax

```
ALTER TABLE {table name}
RENAME CONSTRAINT old constraint name TO new constraint name;
```

SQL Statement

```
ALTER TABLE emp2 RENAME CONSTRAINT ck_emp2_salary TO ck_emp2_min_salary;
```

Remove a Table

To remove a table from the database you use the DROP TABLE command. It is a DDL command which, when issued, permanently deletes the specified table along with all the data in the table. Keep the following points in mind before using this vital command:

- There is no *Are you sure?* confirmation from the database.
- This command is irreversible, which means that once this command executes successfully, you'll permanently lose the table and its data immediately.
- Other dependent objects (views, stored procedures, functions, and so on) will become invalid.
- You cannot drop a table with active referential integrity constraints. For this, you have to use the CASCADE CONSTRAINTS option which also drops dependent integrity constraints.
- The good news is that only the owner of the table or a person provided with relevant privileges can perform this operation.

Syntax
```
DROP TABLE {table name} [CASCADE CONSTRAINTS];
```

SQL Statement
```
DROP TABLE emp5 CASCADE CONSTRAINTS;
```

Test Your Skill

1. A table definition consists of the following four components:

    a. _____ b. _____ c. _____ d. _____

2. Out of the above four table definition components, the following two are mandatory:

    a. _____ b. _____

3. Identify a value which can be stored in a numeric column:
    - a. 'Salary'
    - b. '10,000'
    - c. ' 01-JAN-2015'
    - d. 145.65

4. A character column can accept the following values. Select all that apply.
    - a. 'Salary'
    - b. '10,000'
    - c. '01-JAN-2015'
    - d. 145.65

5. Which data type is used to store digitized data?
   a. Number   c. Date
   b. BLOB   d. VARCHAR

6. Which constraint is used to prohibit null values?

7. The purpose of implementing the UNIQUE constraint is to:
   a. Add Primary Keys
   b. Add Foreign Keys
   c. Prevent duplicate values
   d. Accept null values

8. What constraint would you define for the gender column, and how?

9. What sequence would you follow to create related parent and child tables?
   a. Create child and then the parent table.
   b. Create parent before the child table.

10. In which sequence would you drop related parent and child tables?
    a. Drop parent before the child.
    b. Drop child before the parent.

11. After creating a table you realized a mistake in the name of a column? How would you correct this mistake?

12. Are the following examples syntactically correct?
    a. Create Table Test_1
       (id number(6), name varchar2(30) constraint pk_test_1 primary key(id));

    b. Create Table Orders
       (
       order_id number(6),
       customer_id number(6), constraint nn_ord_cust_id NOT NULL,
       order_total number(12,2),
       dispatched char(1) constraint ck_ord_dispatch CHECK(dispatched IN ('Y','N')),
       constraint pk_ord_id primary key
       );

Manipulate Data In Tables

Chapter 8 – Manipulate Data in Tables

What is Data Manipulation

In database terminology, the term data manipulation signifies toward three major actions, these are: insert, update, and delete. Insert is performed to add new data to the tables, update operation is performed to change the data residing under the tables, and delete helps in removing unneeded data. Once you create a table, you execute these actions using three data manipulation (DML) commands: INSERT, UPDATE, and DELETE.

COMMIT and ROLLBACK

As stated earlier, DDL commands cannot be rolled back; these commands immediately affect the database. In contrast, DML commands (Insert, Update, and Delete) can be reversed using the ROLLBACK command, but prior to using COMMIT. To make the changes permanent and irreversible, use the COMMIT command. On the contrary, to undo the changes as they had never happened, run the ROLLBACK command. These two are also called Transaction Control Statements because they manage changes made by DML statements.

Add Data

The first action that you perform on a table, after its creation, is to add new rows to it. For this, you use the INSERT data manipulation command. This command can be used in the following three ways:

- Add a complete row to a table
- Add a partial row to a table
- Add rows from another table through subquery

The following syntax of the INSERT command is used to add just one row at a time to a table. Use this command when you are inserting either a complete or a partial single row. The third insertion approach is discussed on Page 125.

Syntax

```
INSERT INTO {table name} [(column, column ...)]
VALUES  (value, value ...);
```

Besides the command keywords (INSERT INTO) and the mandatory table name, the above syntax requires column and value information. Note that the column list is optional (hence provided in square brackets). These are the columns in the table that you wish to populate. The VALUE clause is mandatory which holds corresponding values for the columns. It must be provided while inserting a single row, and must be enclosed in parentheses.

Insert a Complete Row

As being optional, you can omit the column list when you are inserting a complete row by adding values for each column in a table. In the following example you are adding a new complete record to the Employees table. Because the statement carries values for each column, therefore the column list is omitted. However, in this kind of manipulation, the values must be listed according to the order of the columns defined in the table. Always enclose character and date values within single quotation marks; don't do so for numeric values. When you do not know a value for a column, just use the null keyword in its place, as it is used for commission percent and manager id columns in the following statement. Omitting it will return "*not enough values*" error message.

The successful execution of this statement will return *1 rows inserted* message in the Script Output pane. Click on the Data tab, and then on the Refresh button under this tab. You'll see this new record. Although inserted, this row is still not permanent in the table. In SQL Develop you can make the change permanent by clicking the commit icon . Alternatively, you can type and execute the COMMIT command in the Worksheet pane. Similarly, click the rollback icon to undo the change, or type and execute the ROLLBACK command.

SQL Statement

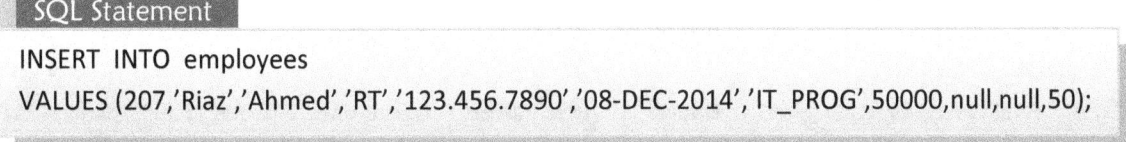

INSERT INTO employees
VALUES (207,'Riaz','Ahmed','RT','123.456.7890','08-DEC-2014','IT_PROG',50000,null,null,50);

Output

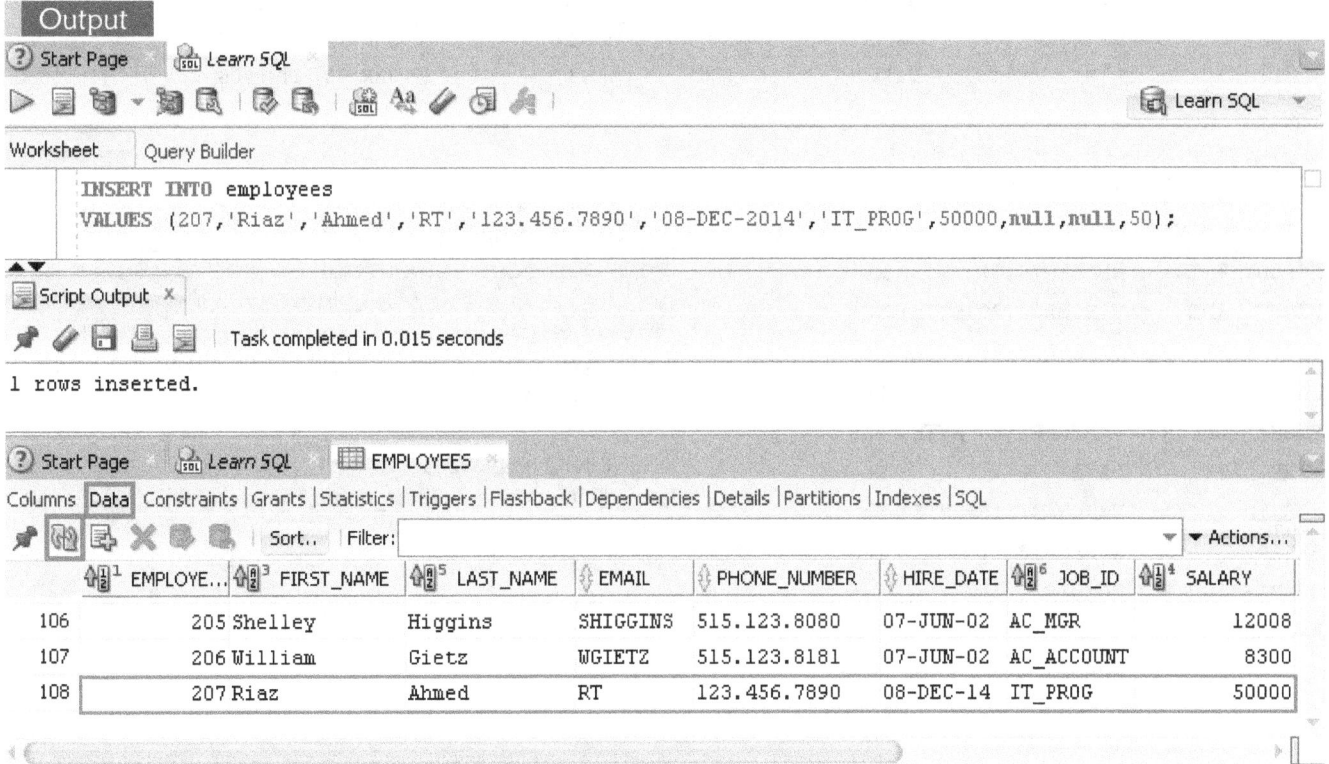

Chapter 8 – Manipulate Data in Tables

Insert a Partial Row

You can also add partial rows to a table which means you only provide values for some specific columns, and not for all. This can be done by explicitly defining the column(s) you wish to populate, as demonstrated in the following statement. In this example, you identified the names of five columns (employee_id, last_name, email, hire_date, and job_id marked as NOT NULLABLE in the table structure) from the Employees table that you intended to populate, and provided corresponding values in the specified column order – the columns left blank here will be filled up in the Update Data section coming ahead. You may omit only those column from such insert operations that allow null values. Omitting a value for a column that does not allow NULL values and does not have a default value as well, will throw an error message, and the row insertion process will fail.

SQL Statement

```
INSERT INTO employees (employee_id, last_name, email, hire_date, job_id)
VALUES (209, 'Sarim', 'SM', '10-DEC-2014', 'IT_PROG');
```

Output

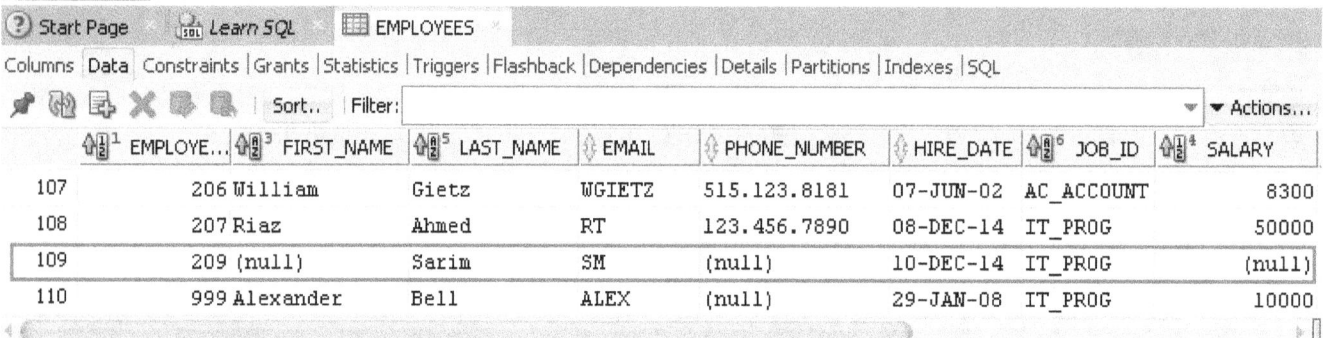

Employees Table Definitions

COLUMN_NAME	DATA_TYPE	NULLABLE
EMPLOYEE_ID	NUMBER(6,0)	No
FIRST_NAME	VARCHAR2(20 BYTE)	Yes
LAST_NAME	VARCHAR2(25 BYTE)	No
EMAIL	VARCHAR2(25 BYTE)	No
PHONE_NUMBER	VARCHAR2(20 BYTE)	Yes
HIRE_DATE	DATE	No
JOB_ID	VARCHAR2(10 BYTE)	No
SALARY	NUMBER(8,2)	Yes
COMMISSION_PCT	NUMBER(2,2)	Yes
MANAGER_ID	NUMBER(6,0)	Yes
DEPARTMENT_ID	NUMBER(4,0)	Yes

> **NOTE**
> In this approach you are not required to follow the column order of the table. Instead, you must provide values according to the list defined in the INSERT statement. For example, you could write this statement like this:
>
> INSERT INTO employees
> (job_id,hire_date,email,last_name,employee_id)
> VALUES
> ('IT_PROG', '10-DEC-2014', 'SM', 'Sarim',209);

Insert Rows from Another Table

In the previous two insert examples you added single rows to the Employees table. There is another form of this command that lets you add multiple rows at once through a subquery. In this form you insert rows into a (target) table from another (source) table. According to the following syntax, you can omit the column list here as well (as done in the first insert example statement below). In this statement you are inserting values from all columns in all rows into a new target table named dept3 from the Departments table.

In the second statement, you specified the columns you wanted to put data in. You also used the WHERE clause in the subquery to set a condition. As you can see in the output screenshot, the statement inserted records of five department (10-50) again. The same records were inserted because there was no primary key constraint defined in the new table.

Couple of things that you must ensure for this particular scenario are that, not only both the source and target tables exist in the same schema, but must also have the same structure. Before you execute the example statements, first execute the statement provided in the side bar to create the target table.

Syntax
```
INSERT INTO {table name} [(column, column ...)]
{subquery};
```

Target Table Statement
```
CREATE TABLE dept3
(
  department_id    number(4),
  department_name  varchar2(30),
  manager_id       number(6),
  location_id      number(4)
);
```

SQL Statement # 1
```
INSERT INTO dept3 SELECT * FROM departments;
```

SQL Statement # 2
```
INSERT INTO dept3 (department_id, department_name)
SELECT  department_id, department_name
FROM    departments
WHERE   department_id <= 50;
```

NOTE
After executing the above CREATE TABLE statement, if the new table didn't appear in the Tables list under the Connections pane, then first click on the Learn SQL connection in this pane, and then click the Refresh icon at the top of this pane.

Output

DEPARTMENT_ID	DEPARTMENT_NAME	MANAGER_ID	LOCATION_ID
30	Purchasing	114	1700
40	Human Resources	203	2400
50	Shipping	121	1500
...	...	...	...
270	Payroll	(null)	1700
10	Administration	(null)	(null)
20	Marketing	(null)	(null)
30	Purchasing	(null)	(null)
40	Human Resources	(null)	(null)
50	Shipping	(null)	(null)

Update Data

While inserting a new record in a previous section you left some columns blank. The UPDATE DML command allows you to fill up null values in table columns as well as replace existing values with new ones. Besides the UPDATE keyword, the syntax of this command has three components:

- **Table Name:** It is the name of the table you want to modify data in.
- **column=value:** The name of the column which is to be modified along with the new value. The (=) operator must be placed in between. You can add more column/value pairs to update as many columns in the table as you want; one pair is mandatory. Each pair must be separated from others with a comma.
- **WHERE condition:** Although optional, the WHERE clause has a very significant role in this command. Here too, you set a condition which determines which rows in the table are to be updated. If you omit this clause, all rows in the table will be updated.

In the following statement, you are updating first name and phone number of employee number 209. Note that in addition to the null values, you can also replace existing values through this command.

Syntax
```
UPDATE  {table name}
SET  {column = value} [, column = value, ...]
[WHERE  condition];
```

> **NOTE**
> Always make a habit to use the WHERE clause in the UPDATE statements, otherwise every row in the table will be updated.

SQL Statement
```
UPDATE employees
SET first_name='Muavia', phone_number='999.999.9999', salary=15000
WHERE employee_id=209;
```

Output

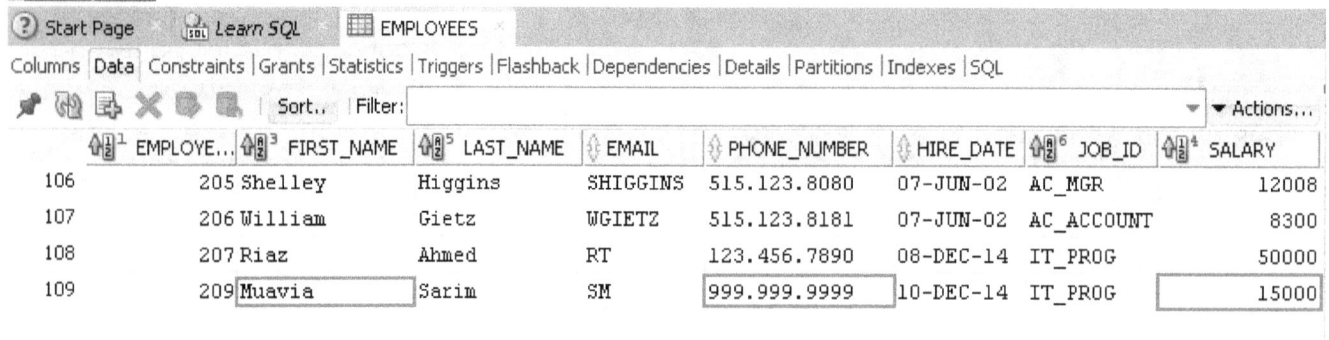

Delete Data

Delete is another important operation which is performed on a database to remove existing rows from a table, and it is performed by executing the DML DELETE command. It also must be used with the WHERE clause, unless you want to delete all records from a table. Use either COMMIT or ROLLBACK to make the changes permanent.

Syntax
```
DELETE FROM {table name}
[WHERE condition];
```

SQL Statement – String Example
```
DELETE FROM employees WHERE first_name='Riaz';
```

SQL Statement – Numeric Example
```
DELETE FROM emp2
WHERE commission_pct > 0 AND job_id <> 'SA_MAN';
```

SQL Statement – Date Example
```
DELETE FROM emp2
WHERE hire_date < TO_DATE('01.01.2001','DD.MM.YYYY');
```

SQL Statement – Delete All Records Example
```
DELETE FROM emp3;
```

SQL Statement – Failure Example
```
DELETE FROM departments WHERE department_id = 10;
```

> **NOTE**
> Always make a habit to use the WHERE clause in the DELETE statements, otherwise every row in the table will be deleted.

The first example, which uses a string condition, deletes a single record, because there is just one row having the first name 'Riaz'. If you have multiple records with the same first name (such as John), then you should add more filters using the AND operator to delete the specific record, as demonstrated in the second example, which removes multiple records, but ensures that the employees working as Sales Manager (who are also eligible to get commissions) are not deleted.

Since there exists no employee who was hired on or before 1st January 2001, the date example will not delete any record.

The next example deletes all rows from the emp3 table.

The last statement attempts to delete department number 10. This statement will fail due to the implementation of the integrity constraint, and will return *integrity constraint (HR.EMP_DEPT_FK) violated - child record found* error. The error occurs because the department number provided in the WHERE clause is referenced by the foreign key constraint declared in the Employees table, which contains record of one employee (Jennifer Whalen) enrolled in this department.

Chapter 8 – Manipulate Data in Tables

Test Your Skill

1. What are the two commands that you execute after performing a DML operation?

2. Identify error in the following statement:
   INSERT INTO Departments VALUES (99,'Manufacturing');

3. Identify errors in the following statement:
   UPDATE Employees first_name=Smith salary=10,000
   WHERE employee_id=999;

4. Do you think that the following statement would execute?
   DELETE FROM Employees
   WHERE hire_date > to_date('01-01-2015');

5. Add a new record to the Employees table. Allocate an used department to this new employee. Insert only required values, and commit the insertion.

6. Attempt to delete the department used in step 5. Was it deleted?

7. Delete the employee created in step 5 and try to delete the department again. What happened this time?

Other Database Objects

Chapter 9 – Other Database Objects

Database Objects

Besides tables and constraints, each schema in a relational database management system can have several other objects. The following list is a subset of those objects that serve some specific functions, and are supported by all major DBMSs.

- Views
- Indexes
- Stored Procedures
- Triggers

What are views?

A view can be defined as a logical table which represents one or more tables or views. A view is nothing more than a stored query. It contains no data of its own. It derives its data from the tables (called base tables) on which it is based. Base tables can be tables or other views. All operations performed on a view actually affect the base tables.

What are Views good for?

- Views prevent direct access to the tables.
- Views restrict full access to the tables by providing selective columns from selective tables.
- Views simplify queries by presenting complex join results using a simple SELECT statement. For example, you can create a single view which fetches data from multiple tables using joins. This view will hide the fact that the information it is delivering actually resides in multiple tables. You can also add extensive calculations in your view. This way the end users can get their desired information without knowing how to create joins or calculations.
- Views present different data to different user groups.
- Views are extremely beneficial for end users who do not know how to write complicated queries.
- Views can format and present data differently from that stored in the base tables. For example, the columns of a view can be renamed without affecting the tables on which the view is based.

Syntax

```
CREATE VIEW {view name} [(column alias, ...)]
AS subquery;
```

> **NOTE**
> Some DBMSs do not allow the ORDER BY clause in views.
>
> Oracle and some other DBMSs use CREATE OR REPLACE VIEW command to modify an existing view.
>
> Use *DROP VIEW {view name}* to remove a view. Dropping views do not affect the tables on which they were based.

Create a View

In the following example a view is created to display department names along with minimum, maximum, and average salaries being paid in each department. After successful execution of the statement, you'll see a message saying "*view VW_DEPT_SALARY created*" in the Script Output pane. You can verify this message by expending the Views node under the Connections section.

SQL Statement to create a view

```
CREATE VIEW   vw_dept_salary (department, minimum, maximum, average)
AS SELECT     d.department_name, min(e.salary), max(e.salary), round(avg(e.salary))
FROM          departments d, employees e
WHERE         d.department_id=e.department_id
GROUP BY      d.department_name;
```

Now that the view is created, you can use it by entering a simple SELECT statement, that follows, in the Worksheet area.

SQL Statement to use a view

```
SELECT * FROM vw_dept_salary;
```

Output

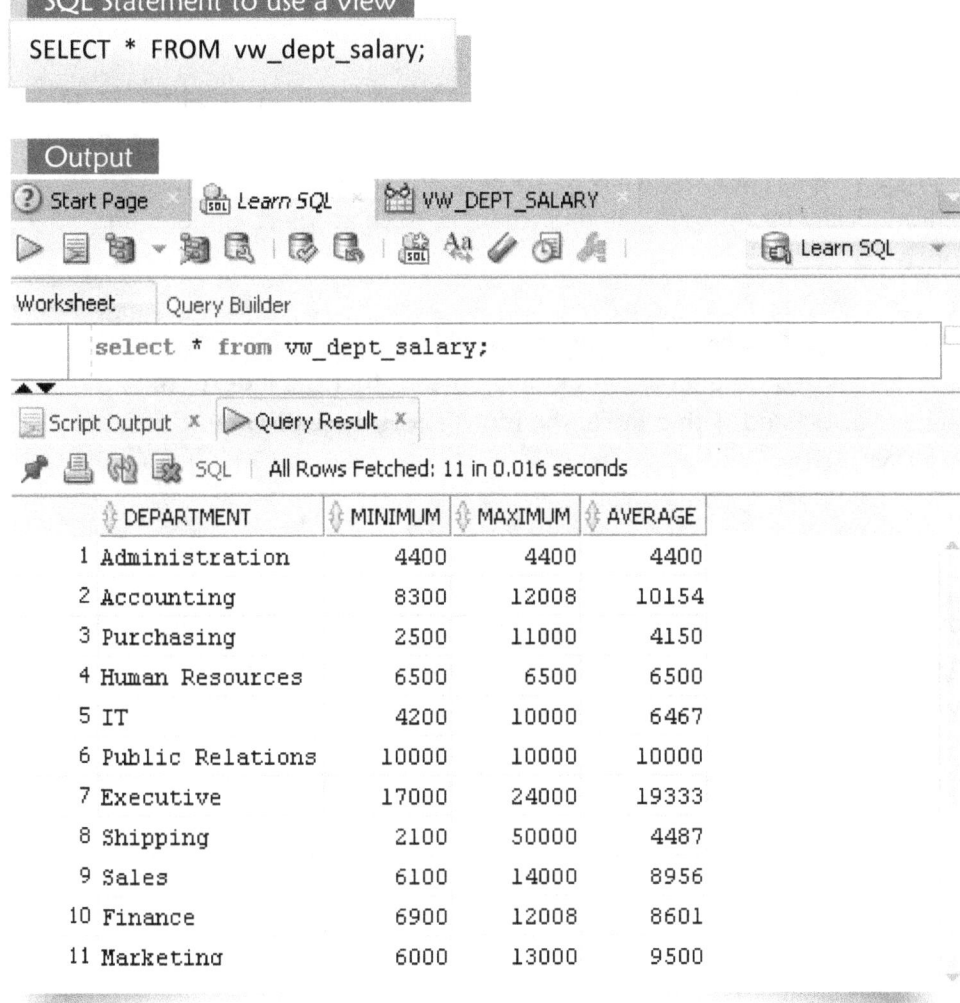

	DEPARTMENT	MINIMUM	MAXIMUM	AVERAGE
1	Administration	4400	4400	4400
2	Accounting	8300	12008	10154
3	Purchasing	2500	11000	4150
4	Human Resources	6500	6500	6500
5	IT	4200	10000	6467
6	Public Relations	10000	10000	10000
7	Executive	17000	24000	19333
8	Shipping	2100	50000	4487
9	Sales	6100	14000	8956
10	Finance	6900	12008	8601
11	Marketing	6000	13000	9500

What are Indexes?

An index is an optional database object which is created on one or more columns of a table. The basic objective of an index is to increase the performance of data retrieval. In the presence of indexes, a database can efficiently locate the requested rows. Indexes are useful when applications often query a specific row or range of rows. Indexes are independent objects which means that you can drop and create indexes with no effect on the tables. In the absence of indexes a full table scan is performed to find a value. For example, without an index, a query of employee number 200 in the Employees table requires the DBMS to search every row in the table for this value. This approach can be feasible for small tables, but is not certainly suitable for large volumes of data.

To elaborate further, let's see an example. You have this book in your hand and want to search all occurrences of the word *schema* in it. What will you do? Definitely, you will go to the index provided at the back of this book to get all the page numbers where this word is used. Now suppose that the book doesn't have the index, then what? In this situation you will search every line of the book to find this word, starting from the first page. Of course, it is a nightmare, and no one would ever like to perform this exercise. This is why books have indexes to make your search easier. Database indexes are created to serve the same purpose. Once you define an index on one or more columns, your DBMS uses this sorted index to find the location of the required information.

An index can be imagined as a fast access path to reach the desired information. It is created to increase the speed of execution. Given a data value that has been indexed, the index points directly to the location of the rows containing that value. Your DBMS automatically looks after and uses the indexes after their creation, and maintains them automatically by reflecting all data changes (such as insert, update, and delete) without user intervention.

You can create more than one index on a table. However, more indexes on a table also come with a side effect. Each DML operation that is committed on a table with indexes means that the indexes must be updated. The more indexes you have associated with a table, the more effort the DBMS must make to update all the indexes after every DML action.

Guidelines

- Create an index on a column which is used frequently in the WHERE clause or in a join condition. Don't create indexes on columns that are not often used as a condition in queries.
- Columns that contain wide range of values (for example, first and last names of employees) are good candidate for it.
- Create indexes for large table.
- Provide a unique name to each index.

SQL for Everyone

Create an Index

The following statement creates an index on the first name column in the Employees table to improve the speed of query access. The successful execution of this statement will show *index EMP_FIRST_NAME_IX created* in the Script Output pane.

Syntax

CREATE INDEX {index name} ON {table name} ({column}, [column, ...]);

SQL Statement

CREATE INDEX emp_first_name_ix ON employees(first_name);

> **NOTE**
> Use DROP INDEX {index name} to remove an index.

Output

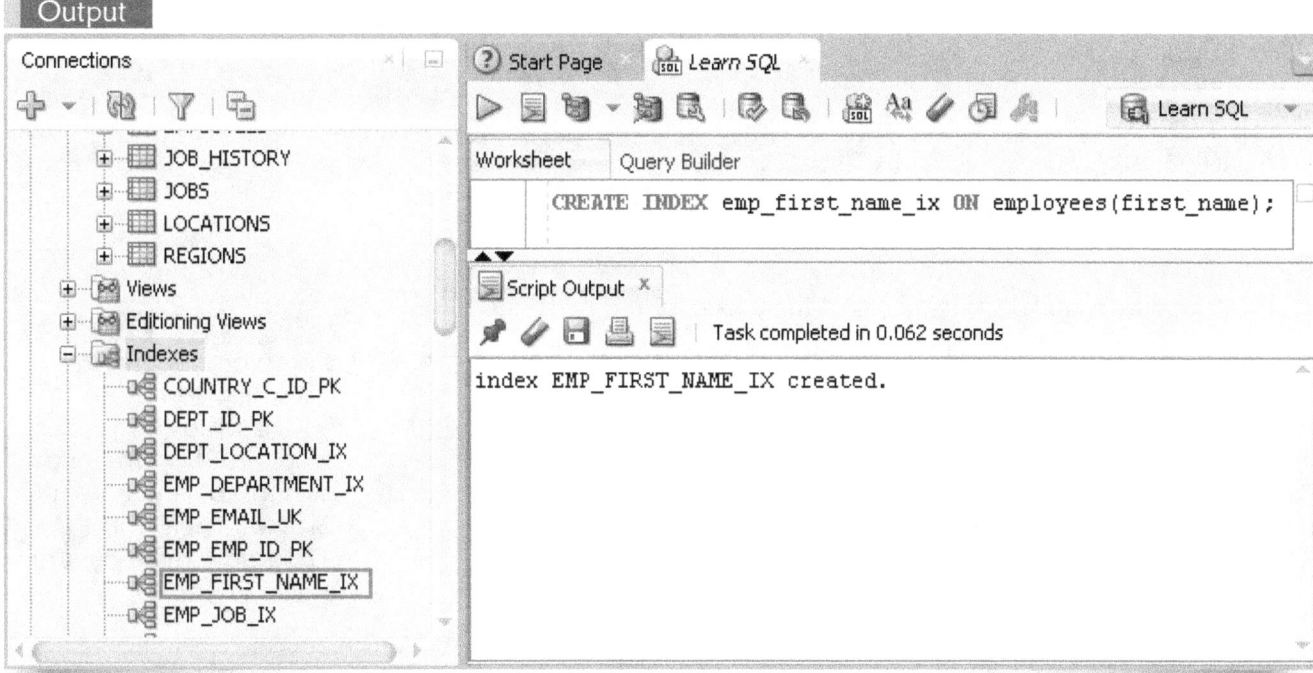

Chapter 9 – Other Database Objects

What are Stored Procedures?

In chapter 7 you learned how to enforce data integrity rules using integrity constraints. However, you cannot enforce business rules with these integrity constraints. To enforce complex business rules all DBMSs (except SQLite) offer an object called stored procedure. A stored procedure is a compiled collection of SQL statements, variable declaration, flow control statements, and so on, that you create and store in a database. With the help of stored procedures you can also enforce complex data integrity because they contain predefined instructions that inform the DBMS what action a user can perform. In other words, a stored procedure is a method of data access that users cannot dynamically change. They add additional level of security to a database, because in the presence of a stored procedure, users never require object privileges (for example, SELECT, INSERT, UPDATE, and DELETE) to access database objects directly; they require only the EXECUTE privilege on the stored procedure to manipulate data.

Syntax

```
CREATE PROCEDURE {procedure name} [(parameter1 IN|OUT|IN OUT data type, parameter2 ...)] IS
   [variable declaration]
BEGIN
   execution block
[EXCEPTION
   exception block]
END [procedure name];
```

Where:

- **Procedure Name:** It is the name of the procedure to be created. Specify OR REPLACE (after the CREATE keyword) to re-create the procedure if it already exists.
- **Parameters:** Specifies the name of an argument to the procedure. If the procedure does not accept parameters, you can omit the parentheses following the procedure name.
- **IN:** Specify IN to indicate that you must supply a value for the parameter when calling the procedure.

> **NOTE**
> Stored procedures are not supported by SQLite and its syntax also varies among DBMSs. The one presented here is from Oracle to help you evaluate it in the current environment.

- **OUT:** Specify OUT to indicate that the procedure passes a value for this argument back to its calling environment after execution.
- **IN OUT:** Specify IN OUT to indicate that you must supply a value for the argument when calling the procedure and that the procedure passes a value back to its calling environment after execution. If you omit IN, OUT, and IN OUT, then the argument defaults to IN.
- **Datatype:** Specify the datatype of the parameter. A parameter can have any datatype defined earlier.
- **IS:** It is a mandatory clause to declare a procedure.
- **Variable Declaration:** If the execution block uses some variables, declare them here.
- **BEGIN:** It's a keyword which signifies the start of the execution block.
- **EXCEPTION:** The code in this block is executed when the main execution block fails. It is usually added for error handling.
- **END:** Marks the end of a procedure.

To understand how stored procedures work, let's create one to enforce a business rule, which says: When a user deletes an employee's record from the Employees table, the DBMS should log into an audit trail table the ID and the name of the deleted employee along with the current date and the computer name from where the delete action initiated. Create this stored procedure using the following steps:

Step # 1   Create Audit Trail Table

Execute the following statement to create a table named Audit Trail, which will be used to store the credentials of the deleted employees.

```sql
CREATE TABLE audit_trail (empid number(6), first varchar2(25), last varchar2(25),
deletedon date, deletedby varchar2(25));
```

Step # 2   Create DeleteEmployee Stored Procedure

Type and execute the following stored procedure in the Worksheet pane. A message saying *PROCEDURE DELETEEMPLOYEE compiled* will indicate that the procedure now resides in your database.

```sql
CREATE OR REPLACE PROCEDURE DeleteEmployee (empid IN Integer) IS
  first varchar2(25);
  last varchar2(25);
  terminal varchar2(20);
BEGIN
  terminal := SYS_CONTEXT('USERENV','HOST');
  SELECT first_name, last_name INTO first, last FROM employees WHERE employee_id=empid;
  INSERT INTO audit_trail VALUES (empid, first, last, sysdate, terminal);
  DELETE FROM employees WHERE employee_id=empid;
  COMMIT;
EXCEPTION
  WHEN NO_DATA_FOUND THEN raise_application_error(-20123,'Invalid Employee ID');
END DeleteEmployee;
```

The procedure receives one parameter (empid) as an integer value from the calling environment – in our case it will be the EXECUTE command that you'll see in step # 3. Next, you declared three variables (first, last, and terminal) to hold the name of an employee, and the client machine from where the delete action was executed. We used Oracle's *SYS_CONTEXT* function to store the name of the client machine in the variable using an assignment operator (:=). The SELECT statement in the execution block stores the name of the employee in the specified two variables. This is another use of the SELECT statement which is utilized in procedures to store table values in variables for further processing. Then comes the INSERT statement, which adds a record to the audit trail table to maintain deletion history. Note that we used the SYSDATE function to record when the delete action was performed. The DELETE statement on the next line removes the record of the specified employee from the EMPLOYEES table. We also used the COMMIT command to make the changes permanent. The code provided in the EXCEPTION block comes into action when you provide an employee id which doesn't exist in the table. To see what this block does, pass 9999 as an argument in the EXECUTE command – which is explained next.

Chapter 9 – Other Database Objects

Step # 3 — Execute the Stored Procedure

To run a stored procedure you type the EXECUTE command, then list the procedure name, followed by the parameter value(s), which are delimited by commas and enclosed in parentheses. Here is its syntax:

Syntax

EXECUTE {procedure name} (parameter value, parameter value, ...);

Run the following command in the Worksheet pane to execute the DeleteEmployee procedure. The EXECUTE command calls the stored procedure by passing a value (employee id) to it. This values goes into the empid parameter (defined as integer in the procedure), which then is used in the SELECT and DELETE statements. After executing this command, you'll see a message *anonymous block completed* in the Script Output pane. Inspect the two affected tables (Employees and Audit Trail). You'll find that the record of employee number 207 is vanished from the Employees table, and a corresponding history record is inserted into the audit table for this employee as shown in the following illustration.

> **NOTE**
> When you create a stored procedure, it is saved in the schema you are currently connected to (for example, HR in the current scenario). Like other database objects, the user HR owns it, and other users cannot execute it unless they are explicitly granted the EXECUTE privilege on the procedure. Here is how it is granted:
>
> GRANT EXECUTE ON DeleteEmployee to {username};

SQL Statement to use a view

EXECUTE DeleteEmployee(207);

> **NOTE**
> Use the following command to remove a procedure from the database.
>
> DROP PROCEDURE {procedure name};

Output

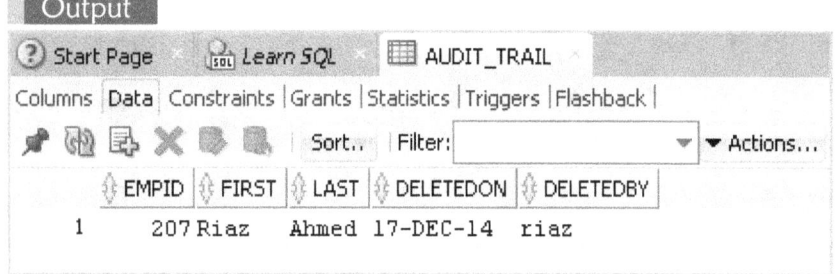

Stored Procedures Advantages

Here are some of the main advantages to using stored procedures:

- Rather than executing single SQL statements, you can put them in a stored procedure to perform complex operations.
- All users can share the same procedure to execute the same set of instructions for recurring tasks, which not only prevents errors, but also ensures data consistency.
- Stored procedures also simplify the process of change management. You need to only change the stored procedure in case a change occurs in your backend database without other users even knowing about the change.

Database Users, schemas, and Privileges

Files that make up the database are stored on a machine called database server. These files are shared by many users. To keep each user's data separate and secure, an account is created for each user that is identified by a unique username and password. Each user account owns tables and other data objects within its area of the database, which is called that user's **schema**.

Usually a DBMS implements two security levels to protect schema objects. The first level controls access to the database itself. To cross this level, you must enter a username and a password. You did not provide these credentials every time when you connected to the database in SQL Developer, because you instructed the software to save this information in chapter 2. The second security level controls what privileges a user possesses once s/he connects to the database. These privileges are split into two categories: **system privileges** and **object privileges**.

System privileges are granted to an individual user to control his operations on the database. For example, connecting to the database or creating a new user or a table fall under this category. New user accounts are created in a database using the following SQL command, where riaz is the username and ahmed is his password.

CREATE USER riaz IDENTIFIED BY ahmed

Object privileges, on the other side, are granted to a user on an individual database object, such as tables. These privileges control how a user can access and manipulate that object. Examples of object privileges on a table include data insertion, deletion, updating, and view.

You can share your schema objects with others by granting object privileges on your schema objects to specified users. For this, you Use the **GRANT** command (as follows) to grant either system or object privileges:

Grant Syntax: GRANT privilege, privilege, ... TO username;
Examples: GRANT CREATE SESSION, CREATE TABLE to riaz;
                 GRANT SELECT,INSERT,UPDATE,DELETE ON Employees to riaz;

Conversely, you can also withdraw the granted privileges any time using the **REVOKE** command.
Examples: REVOKE CREATE TABLE FROM riaz;
                 REVOKE UPDATE,DELETE ON Employees FROM riaz;

Since GRANT and REVOKE commands control access to the database objects, therefore, these two commands fall under the Data Control Language (DCL) category.

Chapter 9 – Other Database Objects

What are Triggers?

The DeleteEmployee stored procedure demonstrated how to use multiple SQL statements to enforce a business rule. If you want to allow users to perform data manipulation actions without a stored procedure, but at the same time also want to automatically enforce the same business rule, then you can use triggers instead.

Database triggers are similar to stored procedures in the sense that they both have the same syntax sections, and both reside in the database. Besides similarities, there are a couple of differences between these two objects. The first difference is that triggers do not accept parameters. They also differ in the way they execute. You already went through a practical example for the stored procedures where you executed it using the EXECUTE command. In contrast, a trigger executes only when a specific event occurs. When a trigger executes, it is said to have fired. DBMS commands (INSERT, UPDATE, and DELETE) can cause triggers to fire. A trigger can fire either before or after its associated SQL command. A BEFORE trigger is often used to grab old values before data manipulation. These values are stored in a table along with new values for auditing purpose. The AFTER trigger is fired after a data manipulation action is performed. For example, you can create an AFTER trigger to update an inventory table after each sale to get current stock position.

Syntax

```
CREATE OR REPLACE TRIGGER {trigger name}
[BEFORE | AFTER] [INSERT | UPDATE | DELETE] ON table name
[FOR EACH ROW]
[DECLARE variable declaration]
BEGIN
  trigger action
[EXCEPTION
  exception block]
END [trigger name];
```

NOTE

To remove a trigger from the database use:

DROP TRIGGER {trigger name};

Just like constraints, you can also enable/disable a trigger like this:

ALTER TRIGGER {trigger name ENABLE | DISABLE}

Step # 1 Create Audit Trail Table

The sample trigger that you are going to create in this section will maintain a log of DML operations performed on the Employees table. Execute the following statement to create a table that will keep track of such user actions.

```
CREATE TABLE audit_employees (empid number(6), actiondate date,
performedby varchar2(25), action char(6));
```

Step # 2 Create Audit_Employees Trigger

Type the following code in the Worksheet pane to create the trigger. After clicking the execute button, you'll see "Enter Binds" dialog box. This box appears to receive values for the provided bind variable (:new and :old). Keep the NULL checkbox provided on this dialog box checked, and click the Apply button to dismiss it. The trigger will be saved in your database with a confirmation message: *TRIGGER AUDIT_EMPLOYEES compiled.*

The trigger is named AUDIT_EMPLOYEE and it will fire for all three DML operations (INSERT, UPDATE, and DELETE) performed on the Employees table. FOR EACH ROW is specified to designate the trigger as a row trigger. DBMS fires a row trigger once for each row that is affected by the triggering statement. We declared two variables (vDateNow and vTerminal) that are used in the beginning of the trigger action area to store current system date and client computer name. Then we used an IF condition block to evaluate the DML operation. The first one checks whether the user inserted a new record. If so, then the insert statement defined on the next line is fired to record the insert operation in the audit table; the other two statements are ignored. The trigger uses three conditions that target the Employees table. The DBMS fires the trigger when someone issues a statement to perform any of the three DML operations for the Employees table. The trigger is executed immediately after performing the DML action. In case of multiple row manipulations with a single statement the trigger fires once for each record. To reference existing and new column values in a trigger body, you use the syntaxes *:OLD.column_name* and *:NEW.column_name*, respectively.

```sql
CREATE OR REPLACE TRIGGER Audit_Employees AFTER INSERT OR UPDATE OR DELETE ON Employees
FOR EACH ROW
DECLARE
  vDateNow DATE;
  vTerminal CHAR(20);
BEGIN
  -- get current time, and the terminal of the user:
  vDateNow := SYSDATE;
  vTerminal := SYS_CONTEXT('USERENV','HOST');
  IF INSERTING THEN
    INSERT INTO Audit_Employees VALUES (:new.employee_id, vDatenow, vTerminal, 'INSERT');
  ELSIF DELETING THEN
    INSERT INTO Audit_Employees VALUES (:old.employee_id, vDatenow, vTerminal, 'DELETE');
  ELSE
    INSERT INTO Audit_Employees VALUES (:old.employee_id, vDatenow, vTerminal, 'UPDATE');
  END IF;
  COMMIT;
END;
```

Step # 3   Fire Trigger

Now that the trigger is created, let's fire it to get the audit trail on the Employees table. Execute the following statements one after the other in the Worksheet area, and watch the two tables – Employees and Audit_Employees.

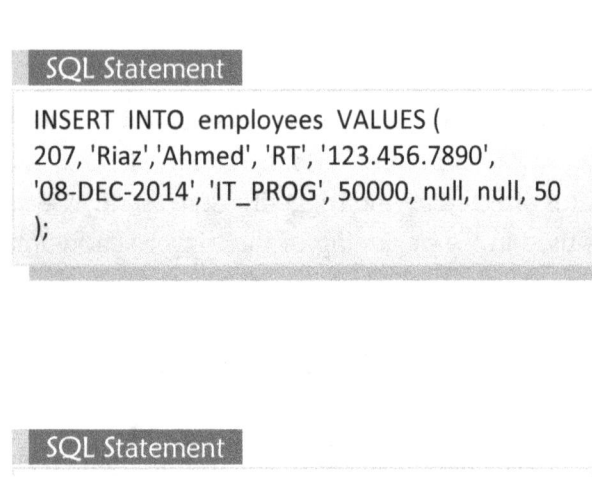
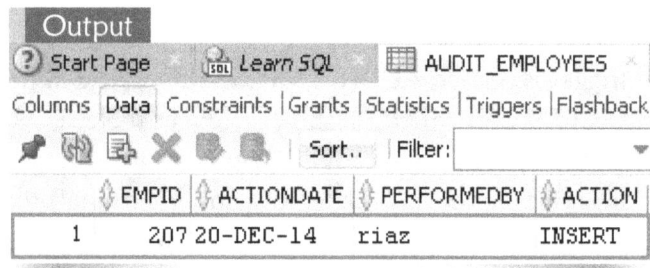

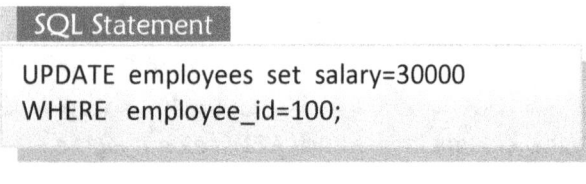
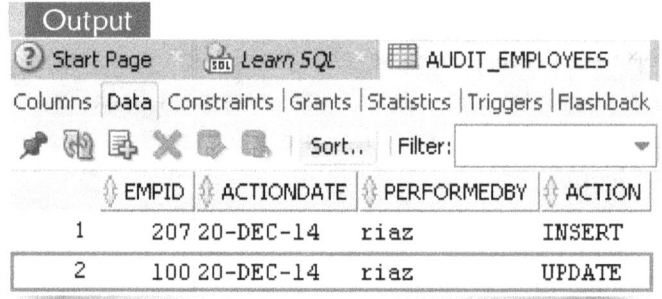

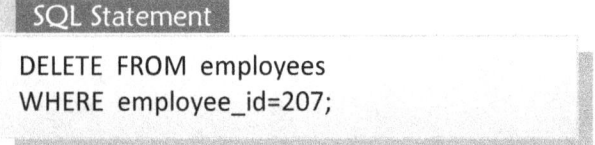
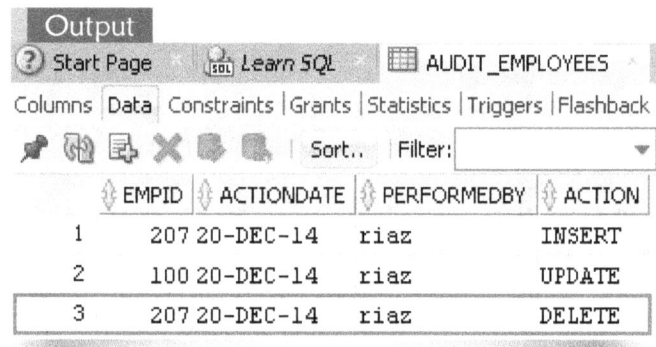

When you execute the first statement above, the DBMS performs two insert operations. First, it adds a complete record to the Employees table with all the values provided in the statement. Then, it logs an entry (as shown in the corresponding output) in the audit table, revealing the action and computer name. Similar log entries are recorded for the update and delete statements.

The example presented in this section is a very simple one to give you a taste of triggers. However, you can create comprehensive triggers that can even keep track of individual updated column values, and can perform various other tasks automatically behind the scenes.

Conclusion

Although the book ends here, your journey to explore the huge world of SQL certainly does not. Besides learning the basics of SQL, you went through some frequently used advanced topics like Joins, Subqueries, Stored Procedures, Indexes, and Triggers in this book.

SQL can be used not only to answer simple questions that you saw throughout this book. Using advanced features of this language you can even perform multidimensional data analysis as well, to answer complex analytical questions. These include ROLLUP, CUBING, RANKING, and WINDOWING to name a few.

You've got the whole world in front of you. Keep your spirits high and move on gradually to become a guru.

Good Luck!

Test Your Skill

1. Which database object is used to prevent direct access to table data?
   a. Indexes
   b. Views
   c. Triggers
   d. Tables

2. Which of the following database object is used to increase data retrieval performance?
   a. Stored Procedures
   b. Triggers
   c. Views
   d. Indexes

3. By passing parameters, which object do you use to enforce complex business rules?
   a. Triggers
   b. Views
   c. Stored Procedures
   d. Constraints

4. What command do you use to invoke a stored procedure?

5. What is the command to fire a trigger?

Answers to Test Your Skills Questions

APPENDIX

Answers: Chapter – 1

1 C   2 B   3 C   4 A   5 A   6 C   7 C   8 B

9 A   10 B   11 C

12: A=DCL   D=DDL   G=DML
     B=DML   E=DML   H=DDL
     C=DDL   F=DCL

13:

Locations	Key	Departments	Key	Employees	Key
location_id	PK	department_id	PK	employee_id	PK
location_name		department_name		employee_name	
		location_id	FK	department_id	FK

Answers: Chapter – 2

1. Microsoft SQL Server, IBM DB2, and MySQL.

2. Location of Java.exe file.

3. SQL Command Line utility under Oracle XE program group.

4. Connection Name, Username, Password, Hostname, Port, and System Identifier (SID).

Answers: Chapter – 3

1. Select * from Locations;

2. Select first_name, salary from Employees;

3. Select salary, first_name from Employees;

4. Yes

5. Yes

6. The expression *salary x 12 Annual Salary* contains two errors. You must use the asterisk character (*) for multiplication and enclose the alias in quotes like this: "Annual Salary". The column name is also not correct is should be *salary*. Finally, the search string used in the LIKE operator must be enclosed in single quotations like this: LIKE '%05'.

7. Select first_name, salary, commission_pct
   From employees
   Where commission_pct is not null;

8. Select first_name||' '|| last_name Employees, department_id
   From Employees
   Where department_id=10 or department_id=20
   Order by last_name;

9. Select * from employees where last_name like '%y%';

10. Select first_name, salary, commission_pct
    From employees
    Where commission_pct is null and department_id=90;

11. Select first_name||' '||last_name Employee, hire_date
    from   employees
    where hire_date between '01-JUL-03' and '30-SEP-03'
    order by hire_date;

12. Select first_name||' '||last_name Employee, salary
    from   employees
    where salary < 3000 or salary > 10000
    order by salary;

13. Select first_name||' '||last_name Employee, salary, department_id
    from   employees
    where department_id in (10,20,30) and salary > 3000
    order by salary;

14. Select last_name,salary,commission_pct,salary*commission_pct*12 "ANNUAL COMMISSION"
    from employees
    where job_id in ('SA_MAN', 'SA_REP')
    order by employee_id;

15. Select first_name||' '||last_name Employee, hire_date
    from   employees
    where hire_date not like '%03'
    order by hire_date;

16. Select distinct department_id from employees order by department_id desc;

17. Select last_name, department_id, salary
    from   employees
    where (department_id=50 or department_id=90) and salary >= 5800;

Answers: Chapter – 4

1. Select employee_id, first_name, round(salary+(salary*10)/100) INCREMENTED_SALARY
   from employees;

2. Select concat(concat(first_name,' '),last_name)||' ['||job_id||']' "Employee and Job ID"
   from employees;

3. Select last_name, to_char(hire_date, 'fmDD "of" Month YYYY') HIRE_DATE
   from employees
   where hire_date like '%03';

4. Select department_name, length(department_name) CHARACTERS
   from departments
   order by department_id;

5. Select first_name Employee, nvl(to_char(manager_id),'No Manager') Manager
   from employees;

6. Select first_name, substr(first_name,2,3) extracted
   from employees;

7. Select first_name||' '||last_name employee,
          to_char(hire_date,'yyyy.dd.mon') hired_on
   from   employees
   where first_name='Jennifer';

8. Select employee_id, hire_date, months_between(sysdate,hire_date) tenure
   from employees
   where months_between(sysdate,hire_date) > 100;

9. Select department_id, job_id, count(*) NUMBER_OF_EMPLOYEES
   from employees
   group by department_id, job_id
   order by department_id;

10. Select job_id, min(salary) minimum_salary
    from employees
    group by job_id
    having min(salary) > 15000;

Answers: Chapter – 5

1. No. It can also be used in HAVING, INTO, and SET clauses.

2. a. A subquery must be enclosed in parentheses.
   b. A subquery must not contain an ORDER BY clause.
   Here is the corrected statement:
   ```
   SELECT    first_name, job_id, department_id
   FROM      employees
   WHERE     department_id = (SELECT department_id
                              FROM   employees
                              WHERE first_name='Adam')
   ORDER BY department_id;
   ```

3. IN or NOT IN

4. Select first_name,last_name,job_id,salary
   from employees
   where salary = (select salary
                   from employees
                   where first_name='Karen' and last_name='Colmenares');

5. Select first_name,department_id,job_id
   from employees
   where department_id in (select department_id
                           from   departments
                           where location_id in (1700,2400));

6. Select employee_id,first_name,salary
   from employees
   where salary > (select avg(salary)
                   from employees);

7. Select first_name,last_name,department_id
   from employees
   where manager_id = (select   employee_id
                       from   employees
                       where first_name='Steven' and last_name='King');

Answers: Chapter – 6

1. Referential Integrity Constraints

2. No

3. No

4. To avoid ambiguity, you will use full qualified column names by prefixing table names to these columns.

5. 4 join conditions

6. Select e.first_name||' '||e.last_name EMPLOYEE,
           d.department_name DEPARTMENT
   from   employees e, departments d
   where   e.department_id = d.department_id;

7. Select e.first_name||' '||e.last_name EMPLOYEE,
           d.department_name DEPARTMENT
   from   employees e, departments d
   where   e.department_id = d.department_id and
           e.first_name='John';

8. Select e.first_name||' '||e.last_name EMPLOYEE,
           d.department_name DEPARTMENT, l.city
   from   employees e, departments d, locations l
   where   l.location_id=d.location_id and
           e.department_id = d.department_id and
           e.commission_pct is not null;

9. Select c.country_id, c.country_name, l.city
   from   countries c INNER JOIN locations l ON c.country_id=l.country_id(+)
   order by c.country_id;

Answers: Chapter – 7

1. Column Name, Data Type, Default Value, and Constraint.

2. Column Name and Data Type.

3. 145.65

4. 'Salary', '10,000', and '01-JAN-2015'

5. BLOB

6. NOT NULL

7. Prevent duplicate values.

8. CHECK(gender IN ('M','F'))

9. Create parent before the child.

10. Drop child before the parent.

11. ALTER TABLE {table name} RENAME COLUMN {column name}

12. Both statements are incorrect. The first one should contain a comma between the last column name and the table constraint, as shown below:

    Create Table Test_1
    (id number(6), name varchar2(30), constraint pk_test_1 primary key(id));

    The second one has two errors. First, the comma between the customer_id column and its NOT NULL constraint should be removed. A column constraint should never be separated like this from its corresponding column. Secondly, the table constraint (pk_ord_id) is missing the referenced primary key column i.e. order_id. Here is the correct statement:

    Create Table Orders
    (
      order_id number(6),
      customer_id number(6) constraint nn_ord_cust_id NOT NULL,
      order_total number(12,2),
      dispatched char(1) constraint ck_ord_dispatch CHECK(dispatched IN ('Y','N')),
      constraint pk_ord_id primary key(order_id)
    );

Answers: Chapter – 8

1. COMMIT or ROLLBACK

2. You must provide a list of column if you are not inserting values into all columns. In this statement you are not populating the LOCATION_ID column, therefore, the statement should be passed like this:
   INSERT INTO Departments (department_id,department_name)
   VALUES (99,'Manufacturing');

3. a. The SET clause is missing.
   b. Smith should be enclosed in single quotes.
   c. Comma is missing between the two columns.

   Here is the correct statement:
   UPDATE Employees SET first_name='Smith',salary=10,000 WHERE employee_id=999;

4. No, it will return an error because the format mask in the TO_DATE function is missing. Here is the correct statement:
   DELETE FROM Employees WHERE hire_date > to_date('01-01-2015','DD-MM-YYYY');

5. The insert statement is:

   INSERT INTO Employees (employee_id,last_name,email,hire_date,job_id,department_id)
   VALUES (210,'FRANKLIN','FR',TO_DATE('01-01-2015','MM-DD-YYYY'),'HR_REP',270);

6. In step 5, you used department number 270 for the new employee. The foreign key constraint (EMP_DEPT_FK), implemented in the Employees table, would not allow you to delete this department.

7. After deleting the employee's record the department record was also deleted.

Answers: Chapter – 9

1. Views
2. Indexes
3. Stored Procedures
4. EXECUTE
5. There is no command to fire a trigger. It is fired automatically before or after the associated DML statement.

ABOUT THE AUTHOR

Riaz Ahmed is an IT professional with more than 23 years experience. He started his career in early 90's as a programmer, and has been employed in a wide variety of information technology positions, including analyst programmer, system analyst, project manager, data architect, database designer and senior database administrator. Currently he is working as head of IT for a group of companies. His core areas of interest include web-based development technologies, business intelligence, and databases. Riaz possesses extensive experience in database design and development. Besides all versions of Oracle, he has worked intensively in almost all the major RDBMS on the market today. During his career he designed and implemented numerous databases for a wide range of applications, including ERP. In addition to the best-selling title *Create Rapid Web Applications Using Oracle Application Express* (two editions), he has authored *Implement Oracle Business Intelligence, The Web Book – Build Static and Dynamic Websites*, and *SQL for Everyone*. You can reach him through: realtech@cyber.net.pk

Implement Oracle Business Intelligence

**Analyze the Past
Streamline the Present
Control the Future**

http://www.amazon.com/
Implement-Oracle-Business-Intelligence-Volume/dp/1475122012

The Web Book
Build Static and Dynamic Websites

The ultimate resource to building static and dynamic websites

http://www.creating-website.com

Create Rapid Web Applications Using
Oracle Application Express – Second Edition

A practical guide to rapidly develop professional web & mobile applications

http://www.amazon.com/
Create-Applications-Oracle-Application-Express/dp/1492314188

INDEX

Symbols

; semicolon 16
[] square brackets 16
{} curly brackets 16
* asterisk 16-17
| vertical bar 16
|| concatenation operator 23,47
() parentheses 21,31
' single quotation 33-123
-- inline comments 42
/* */ multi-line comments 42

= is equal to 30,86
<>, !=, ^= not equal to 30,86
\> greater than 30,86
\>= greater than or equal to 30,86
< less than 30,86
<= less than or equal to 30,86
% (in LIKE Operator) 36-37
_ (underscore in LIKE Operator) 36-37
(+) Outer Join 98
:= assignment operator 135

A

Abbreviate SQL Commands 16
ADD Clause 113
ADD_MONTHS Function 60
Aggregate Functions 46,70,78
    nesting 75
    used together 77
Alias 16,22,96
ALTER Command 6,8
    ALTER TABLE command 113-118
    ALTER TRIGGER command 138
AND Operator 30,39-41
    precedence rule 41
    used to form multiple subqueries 89
ANSI 2,22,63,97
Arithmetic Operators 19
    apply on dates 69
    precedence 20-21
AS Keyword 22,112
ASC (Ascending) Clause 16,29
Audio Data 103
Audit Trail 135
Average Function – AVG 46,70-72,77,131

B

BETWEEN ... AND ... Operator 30,32,34,58
Bind Variables 139
BLOB Data Type 103
Business Rules 5,138

C

CASCADE Clause 117-119
CAST() Function 63
CHAR Data Type 103,113
Character Functions 46

Character String 5,46
    convert to number/date 63,67-68
    evaluate length 49
    evaluate min/max 75
    fetch specific characters 52
    specify date as 62
    store fixed/variable length strings 103
    transform 48,50-51,53
    using in SQL statements 31,33
CHECK Constraint 5,110
Column 3
    add custom headings 16,22
    add new column 113
    constraint 104-105
    data type 5,102
    default value 104
    defined 4,7
    delete column 113,115
    fetch selected columns data 18
    integrity constraint 5
    join 23-24
    modify column definitions 113-114
    modify values 6
    qualify 95-96
    rename column in table 113,115
    rename in views 130
    select all columns from a table 16
Comments in SQL Statement 42
COMMIT Command 122-123,127,135
Comparison Operators 16,30,32
    multiple row comparison operators 86,88
    precedence rules 31
    single row comparison operators 86
Composite Key 4,107
CONCAT() Function 24,47
Concatenation Operator (||) 23,47
Conditions in SQL Statement *(see WHERE clause)*
CONNECT Command 10

INDEX

CONSTRAINT Clause 117
Constraints (see Data Integrity Constraints)
Conversion Functions 46,63
COUNT function 46,70,73,77-78
CREATE Command 6,8
    CREATE INDEX command 133
    CREATE PROCEDURE command 134-135
    CREATE TABLE command 104,111-112,125,138
    CREATE TRIGGER command 138-139
    CREATE USER command 137
    CREATE VIEW command 130-131
Create Database Objects 6
CURRENCY Data Type 103
Custom Arithmetic Expressions 19

-D-

Data 3
    add new 122
    analysis 70
    change/modify/update 122,126,132
    change presentation using views 130
    compliance 5
    delete 122,127,132
    extract 16
    fetch from selected columns 18
    filtering 32
    grouping 70
    increase retrieval performance 132
    make permanent 122-123
    manipulation 122
    reverse 122-123
    select all 17
    sorting 29
    store 7
    summarize 70,78
Data Control Language (DCL) 5-6,8,137
Data Definition Language (DDL) 5-6,8,104,113,119
Data Integrity Constraints 4,134
    add constraint 113,116
    defined 105
    constraint types 5
    drop constraint 113,117
    enable/disable 118
    implement 5
    rename constraint 113,118
    types 5,105,112
    user defined 5
Data Manipulation Language (DML) 5-6,8,122,126-127,132,138-139
Data Query Language (DQL) 5-6,8
Data Type 5,8,102
    convert 46,63
    defined 103

Database 2
    basic concepts 2-3
    browse objects 11
    change content 6
    connection dialog box 13
    control access 6
    defined 3,7
    execute reports 11
    interact with 5,14
    maintain consistent state 5
    objects 3,6,130
    object privileges 136-137
    query 11,16
    run scripts 11
    security levels 137
    server 137
    system privileges 137
    users 137
Database Management System (DBMS) 2-3
DATE Data Type 103
Date/Time Data 5,31
    calculate 69
    compare data values 56
    compute intervals between dates 46,56
    convert to character string 62-63,65
    current system date 56
    data types 64
    date elements 64
    default format 34,56,64
    evaluate min/max 74
    format 64-65
    functions 46,56,59-62
    manipulation functions 57
DB2 (see IBM DB2)
DECIMAL Data Type 103
DELETE Command 6,8,122,127
    grant privilege 137
    prevent accidental deletion 105
Delete Database Objects 6
DISTINCT Clause 16,27-28,71
DROP Clause 115,117
DROP Command 6,8
    DROP INDEX command 133
    DROP PROCEDURE command 136
    DROP TABLE command 119
    DROP TRIGGER command 138
    DROP VIEW command 130
DESC (Descending) Clause 16,29
DUAL Table 54,56
Duplicate
    prevent duplicate values 4,27-28

INDEX

-E-
Embedded SQL 5
Entity Integrity Constraint 5
Equijoin 95-96
Error
    in INSERT 123-124
    in stored procedures 134
    in subquery 88
    integrity constraint 127
EXECUTE Command 134-136
Execute SQL Statements *(see SQL Statements)*
EXIT Command 10
Expressions 16,32
    arithmetic 19

-F-
Fill Mode (fm) 65
Filter Data 32,80
Foreign Key
    constraint 108-109
    defined 4,7-8
    Referential constraint 5
    in tables 102
FROM Clause 16
Full Qualified Column Names 96
Functions 46
    nesting 47

-G-
GRANT Command 6,8,136-137
Grant Privilege on Database Objects 136
Graphical User Interface (GUI) Software 5,11,16
GROUP BY Clause 16,78-79
    used with WHERE clause 80

-H-
HAVING Clause 16,78,80-82
    add subquery to 86,90

-I-
IBM DB2 2,11
    CURRENT DATE Function 56
    joining columns 24
Image Data 103
IN Comparison Operator 30,35,86,88
Indent SQL Statements 16
Indexes 3,130
    create 133
    defined 132
INITCAP Function 47

Inline Constraint *(see column constraint)*
Inner Join 95,97
INSERT Command 6,8,122-125
    grant privilege 137
INTEGER Data Type 103
Integrity Constraint Types *(see Data Integrity Constraint)*
    defined 105
Interactive SQL 5
INTO Clause
    add subquery to 86
IS NULL Operator 30,38

-J-
Java 5
Java Development Kit (JDK) 11
Joins vs. Subqueries 99
Joining Columns 23-24
Joining Tables 95,102

-L-
LAST_DAY Function 62
Left Join 99
LENGTH Function 49
LIKE Operator 30,36-37
Linux 11
Logical Operators 30
    precedence rules 31
LOWER Function 50

-M-
Mac OSX 11
MariaDB 2
    CURDATE() Function 56
    joining columns 24
    NOT Operator 31
    SUBSTRING() Function 52
    YEAR() Function 58
Matching columns 4
Maximum function – MAX 46,70,74-75,77,131
Microsoft Access 2,11
    DATEPART() Function 58
    DISTINCT clause in aggregate functions 71
    joining columns 24
    LEN() Function 49
    LIKE operator 36
    MID() Function 52
    NOW() Function 56
    UCASE() Function 53

INDEX

Microsoft SQL Server 2,11
    DATALENGTH() Function 49
    DATEPART() Function 58
    GETDATE() Function 56
    joining columns 24
    SUBSTRING() Function 52
    table rename procedure 116
Minimum function – MIN 46,70,74-75,77,131
MODIFY Clause 114
Modify Database Objects 6
MONEY Data Type 103
MONTHS_BETWEEN Function 59
Multiple Row Comparison Operators *(see Comparison Operators)*
MySQL 2,11
    CURDATE() Function 56
    joining columns 24
    SUBSTRING() Function 52
    YEAR() Function 58

-N-

Nesting Aggregate Functions 75
NEXT_DAY Function 61
NOT NULL Constraint 105,114,124
NOT Operator 30-31,86
NULL 4-5
    defined 25
    handling null values 51
    replace 26
NUMBER Data Type 103
Number Elements 66
Numeric Data 5,31,35
    conversion 46,63,66
Numeric Functions 46,54-55
NVL Function 26,51

-O-

Object Privilege 137
ON Clause 97
ON DELETE CASCADE Clause 108
OR Operator 30,39-41
    precedence rule 41
    used to form multiple subqueries 8
Oracle 2,11,13
    connect 10,12,14
    default date 64
    download, install, and test 10
    SYSTEM user 10
Operating Systems 11
ORDER BY Clause 16,29
    in subquery 86
    in Views 130

Out-of-line Constraint *(see table constraint)*
Outer Join 95,98

-P-

Parameters 134-136,138
Password 137
    HR 13
    SYSTEM user 10
PostgreSQL 2
    CURRENT_DATE Function 56
    DATE_PART() Function 58
    joining columns 24
Port Number 10
Precedence Rules
    AND/OR operators 41
    arithmetic operators 21
    comparison/logical operators 31
Presentation Order 16
Primary Key
    constraint 107
    defined 4,7-8
    drop 117
    Entity integrity constraint 5
    in tables 102
    vs. UNIQUE Key 106

-Q-

Query
    data 6,8,11
    outer 86
    results 12

-R-

REAL Data Type 103
REFERENCES Clause 108-109
Referential Integrity Constraint 5,94
RENAME COLUMN Clause 115
RENAME CONSTRAINT Clause 118
RENAME TO Clause 116
Retrieve Data *(see Query Data)*
REVOKE Command 6,8,137
Right Join 99
ROLLBACK Command 122-123,127
ROUND Function 54

INDEX

Row 3
    add complete row 122-123
    add multiple rows 125
    add new row 6,102
    add partial row 122,124
    add rows from another table 122,125
    add single row 125
    count total rows in a table 70,73
    defined 4,7,102
    delete 6,102,127
    divide into groups 16,70,78
    filter 32
    prevent accidental deletion 105,108
    query 102
    search 34
    sorting 29
    update 6,102
Run Statement 12,17

-S-

Schema 3,7,137
    HR (sample schema) 13,17
    share 137
    specify in CREATE TABLE Command 104
    SYS 54
Search Records 34
    with unknown values 36
Security Levels 137
SELECT Command 6,8,16
    grant privilege 137
    statement 17-18
    Syntax 16
SET Clause
    add subquery to 86
    UPDATE statement 126
Single Row Comparison Operators (see Comparison Operators)
Single Row Functions 46
Sorting 29
Space vs. NULL 25,38
Spreadsheet 3,7
SQL
    acronym 2
    background 2
    basic concepts 2
    command categories 5
    command prompt 5,10
    defined 5
    usage 5

SQL Developer 5,10
    browse all tables and structures 12
    connect to Oracle database 12-14
    database connection dialog box 13
    download and install 11
    interface 12
    save connection 13
    start 11
    supported DBMS 11,14
    test connection 13
    using semicolon 16
SQL Statement
    add comments 42
    enter 13
    guidelines 16
    nesting 86
    run/execute 12,17
    see result 12
SQL Worksheet 12-13
SQLite 2
    DATE() Function 56
    joining columns 24
    renaming table 116
    Right Outer Join 99
    stored procedure support 134
    strftime() Function 58
Stored Procedure 6,130
    create 135
    defined 134
    execute 136
    remove 136
Subquery 86
    add rows into table 122,125
    downside 99
    error 88
    in CREATE TABLE command 112
    in HAVING clause 90
    multiple row subquery 88
    multiple subqueries in a statement 89
    single row subquery 87
    vs. Joins 99
SUBSTR Function 52
SUM Function 46,70,76-77
Suppress Duplicate Values 16,27-28
Sybase Adaptive Server 11
System Privilege 137
SYSTEM User Password 10
SYS_CONTEXT Function 135
SYSDATE Function 56,59-62,69,135

INDEX

-T-
Tab (in SQL Statements) 16
Table 3-4,6-7,13
    add new rows 6
    alias 96
    child/parent concept 108
    constraint 104-105
    count records 73
    create 104,111-112
    defined 102
    definition/structure 102
    delete 119
    delete rows 6
    DUAL table 54,56
    join 95
    modify 113
    naming guidelines 104
    relationship 4,7,102
    rename 113,116
    restrict full access 130
    retrieve all data 17
    see data 12
    see structures/definitions 12
    update column values 6
    using proper data types 103
Text data *(see Character String)*
Time Elements 64
Time Format 64
Timestamp 64
TO_CHAR(datetime) Function 63,65
TO_CHAR(number) Function 63,66
TO_DATE Function 63,68
TO_NUMBER Function 63,67
Triggers 3,6,130
    create 139
    defined 138
    fire 140
TRUNC Function 55

-U-
Undo Changes 123
UNIQUE Constraint 106,113
    drop 115,117
UPDATE Command 6,8,122,126
    grant privilege 137
UPPER Function 33,53
User Defined Integrity Constraint 5
Users 6
    SYSTEM user 10
Username 13,137

-V-
VALUE Clause 122
Values 32
    prevent duplicate values 4,27-28
    store old values for audit purpose 138
    store table values in variables 135
    suppress duplicates 16,27-28
VARCHAR2 Data Type 103
Variables 134-135
    bind variable 139
Video Data 103
Views 3,6
    create 131
    defined 130

-W-
WHERE Clause 16
    add subquery to 86
    DELETE statement 127
    filter data 32
    syntax 32
    UPDATE statement 126
    used with GROUP BY 80
    using comparison/logical operators 30
Windows Operating System 10,11

-Z-
Zero vs. NULL 25,38
    replacing null with zero 51